I0797293

THE SOUP SOLUTION

THE SOUP SOLUTION

80 simple recipes for really good soup

Charlotte Pike

Photography by Danielle Wood

Contents

Introduction
7

1 Quick
18

2 No-Cook
36

3 Budget
50

4 Just What the Doctor Ordered
72

5 Winter Warmers
98

6 Oven-Baked
122

7 Finishing Touches
138

8 Building Blocks
158

Index
168

UK–US Glossary
174

Acknowledgements
175

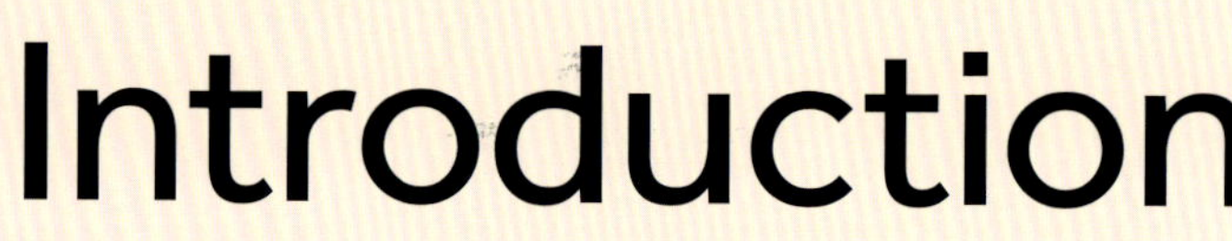

Introduction

I firmly believe that everyone's culinary repertoire should include a collection of great soup recipes. In this book, I want to show you how special soup is and to help you master making fantastic soups at home.

Making great soup from scratch is, I think, such an important life skill. If you can make a soup then you can nourish yourself and others – even if you don't have much equipment, space or time at your disposal. Whether you're cooking for one or a crowd, or you want to eat more healthily or reduce the cost of your weekly shop or use less energy or, simply, you need an easy meal, soup can offer the solution.

The brilliant thing about soup is that it's suitable for all occasions and all tastes. It's generous, welcoming, frugal, comforting, luxurious ... and entirely portable. Homemade soup is pretty much guaranteed to be a feel-good meal, whether it's vegetarians or meat-eaters, adults or children you are feeding.

What's more, one of the best things we can all do for our physical and mental health is to cook more meals from scratch using fresh, nourishing ingredients. Making and eating soup is a really special act of care for yourself and others. I'm confident you'll be amazed by just how good homemade soup tastes and pleasantly surprised at how little it can cost, particularly when compared with a shop-bought equivalent.

This book will provide you with a range of game-changing recipes to suit many occasions and all seasons. I will explain how to get the best results from simple ingredients and how to produce delicious meals that offer solutions to many of the daily challenges we all face when it comes to putting food on the table, whether it's lunch on the go, supper for one or the first course of a dinner party. My recipes include some familiar favourites as well as many you may have never tried before but, hopefully, all of them you will want to make time and time again.

All the soups use easily sourced ingredients and are made using simple techniques that require little in the way of kitchen gadgets. Do be sure to read my tips, tricks and advice to help you get the very best from the soups you make.

There is specific guidance for each recipe on serving, storing and freezing options, so you can plan which ones to make ahead, ready to reheat when you need good food fast. Some are especially useful soups for weekend cooking to last for the week, ideal for packed lunches or days out. I've added a useful key next to each recipe to highlight the following:

vegetarian

no need to blend

make in advance to reheat later

Now to introduce you to The Soup Solution *chapters. Each one is curated with a purpose, to help you choose a soup to match your requirements.*

1 Quick

First, the Quick chapter is designed to do what it says – you'll find a selection of soups to make when time is short. From noodle broths to creamy chowder, these recipes are particularly useful to have up your sleeve for busy days or situations where you need to make an impromptu meal. They are all straightforward to make from scratch and produce truly tasty results in about as little time as it's possible to take. I would say most of these recipes can be made from start to finish in around 20 minutes, and some will take less time than this.

2 No-Cook

In the No-Cook chapter, you'll find a selection of chilled soups that require no cooking, just chopping, blending and chilling. If you haven't eaten chilled soups such as gazpacho or watermelon and cucumber, in warm weather, you're in for a treat. They are one of the most cooling, refreshing and tantalisingly delicious meals to serve on a hot day. While most do require a blender for best results, all the recipes are extremely easy to make.

3 Budget

The Budget chapter showcases particularly inexpensive soups that still deliver on flavour. I've included recipes that feature ingredients that are especially good value and yield generous quantities from comparatively little – ideal for when you need to conjure something out of next to nothing. Whether it's creamy potato or carrot and coriander seed, they all produce really special and delicious results.

4 Just What the Doctor Ordered

In terms of wellbeing, soup is as soothing and nourishing as it gets. The chapter Just What the Doctor Ordered features soups that are particularly comforting and wholesome, for fortifying our general health and for those days when a hug in a bowl is needed. From chicken broth to beetroot and ginger, these are soups packed with health-giving ingredients, such as spinach, turmeric, beans and a wide range of vegetables, to restore our bodies, both physically and mentally.

5

Winter Warmers

Winter Warmers are particularly substantial soups, for cold months or days when you have some hungry mouths to feed. Whether it's a bowl of ramen or spicy cauliflower, the recipes in this chapter are for soups that are a meal in themselves. These are what I make when I really need warming up, especially after a long stretch outdoors.

6

Oven-Baked

The Oven-Baked chapter contains some of my absolute favourites. Roasting chopped veg to make a soup base can save time, effort and energy. Whether it's squash or root veg, once roasted, you simply blend everything with hot stock. This method for preparing soup is a revelation: an ideal, hands-off way of batch cooking to get ahead or to take advantage of spare capacity in the oven when it's already being used for another dish. Oven-baking ingredients dovetails brilliantly into my way of cooking at home, and with very little planning you can become super-organized at making fantastic soups with very little extra effort.

7

Finishing Touches

Finishing Touches contains some truly special and useful ideas for swirls, toppings and accompaniments to elevate your meal and to present your soups with style. From croutons to crispy chilli oil, almost all of them can be made ahead and stored. I am especially fond of the delicious breads and bakes to accompany soups – they are serious crowd-pleasers.

8

Building Blocks

Building Blocks contains a selection of useful recipes to help you make better soup, such as stocks and soup bases. All the recipes can be made in advance and chilled or frozen. The soup base recipes are absolutely game-changing and can be batch-cooked or prepared in advance and frozen until required.

Tips & Tricks

- Seasoning is one of the most important things to get right when making soups. If you use stock cubes, they will be seasoned, so add less salt.
- When you use onions as the base of a soup, allow them time to cook down until they are soft and tender. Adjust the heat level to low–medium to avoid them browning or colouring, which can add a bitter flavour. This applies to garlic, too.
- Adding a pinch of salt to onions as they cook down encourages them to release water and cook more quickly. It also helps to balance the flavour by locking in some seasoning at the outset, rather than adding it all at the end.
- Don't discard the rinds of Parmesan or Parmigiano Reggiano cheese: add them to your soup bases for extra flavour.
- Feel free to add white pepper to some soups, instead of black. This is a trick chefs use, not just for its particular flavour, but also because the pepper flecks are invisible in light-coloured or clear soups.
- You may wish to bring a soup mix to the boil to cook the ingredients, but always reduce the heat to a simmer as soon as it reaches this point – boiling will affect the flavour. This also applies to reheating soups – allow them to come to a simmer but never boil.
- For blended soups, there's no need to chop your vegetables too neatly, as it won't show in the end result. If you find chopping difficult, there is the option of buying frozen, chopped onions as well as other vegetables. Likewise, you can add whole spices to the recipe – they will cook and then be ground up with the additional ingredients. This saves on toasting and grinding spices separately.
- If you intend to add cream, yogurt or coconut milk to a hot soup, aim to use full-fat products wherever possible. Reduced-fat versions tend to split when warmed, resulting in a slightly curdled appearance. Take care to reheat any creamy soups over a very gentle heat.
- When blending soups, always ensure the heat is turned off from the pan and allow the liquid to cool a little first.
- If using a hand-held stick or immersion blender, ensure you allow the blades to come to a complete stop before lifting the blender from the soup. Turn off the power as soon as possible and always before touching or scraping the blades, if needed.
- If using a standalone blender, carefully pour the slightly cooled soup into the jug. Ensure you keep the lid on and fully pressed down, ideally using a tea towel or oven glove, while the blender is running. Applying a little pressure to the lid while the machine is running can help to prevent the lid blowing off – this can occasionally happen with some models if the lid doesn't clip or screw into place.
- Always blend for longer than you think to ensure the silkiest of results.
- If you don't have a blender, provided your vegetables are cooked until really soft, you could use the traditional method of pressing them through a strong sieve with the back of a spoon.
- When roasting soup ingredients, line the tray with a sheet of nonstick baking paper to help save on washing-up later on.

- Ensure cold soups are served chilled. They are best chilled for an hour or two before serving. Feel free to add ice cubes to bowls as you serve the soups, too.
- Generally, soups taste and look better when they are slightly thinner in texture. Use the amount of liquid stated in each recipe as a guide and adjust to get the texture you like best.
- If, however, you feel your soup is too liquid, simmer with the lid off until it reduces down a little. Other tricks to thicken a soup include stirring in a little cornflour mixed to a paste with cold water, or some ground almonds or ground rice, then cooking for a little longer.
- If you find you have oversalted your soup, just peel a potato, cut it in half and put into the soup. It will soak up some of the salt from the liquid. Discard the potato pieces before serving.

Essential Equipment

- A large, lidded, deep-sided saucepan or stockpot is the key item for soup-making. I usually recommend a larger-sized pan – say, 6 litres (10½ pints) – to give you plenty of room to work and also the capacity to scale up the quantities, should you wish to batch-cook.
- A hand-held stick or immersion blender is the easiest and quickest way of blending a soup. Use it directly into the pan (off the heat) and blend, although take great care with hot liquids. Keep the blades submerged while the blender is in action, otherwise you risk flicking the contents out of the pan.
- A stand-alone blender costs more than a stick blender and takes up space in your kitchen but it will achieve the smoothest result. Alternatively, a cheaper, but still effective, option is a hand-operated food mill or mouli-légumes, which will finely purée the ingredients and give you the desired smooth result.
- One or two frying pans, preferably nonstick
- Mixing bowls
- Roasting trays

Useful Kit

- Sieve or colander
- Ladle
- Wooden spoon
- Spatula
- Funnel (handy for filling flasks)
- Soup flasks (see page 14)
- Jug
- Freezerproof containers

Ingredients

Here are some useful ingredients to have to hand for successful soup-making. As with all food, buying the best quality you can afford makes a difference.

Stock: Your Secret Weapon

A well-flavoured stock is the true heart of so many soups, and making your own is incredibly easy. It's a great way to use up all the trimmings and peelings from root vegetables (I store mine in the freezer until I have a batch), the stems from herbs, plus a few pantry ingredients, such as peppercorns and bay leaves.

When preparing stock from scratch, it's important not to add salt to the stock itself, only to the soup you make with the stock, which will help to balance the flavour.

I wholeheartedly recommend making a broth from beef bones or a chicken carcass left over after a roast dinner. Slow simmering extracts all the goodness from the bones: too tasty to waste!

While many of the soups in this book are designed to be vegetarian-friendly, if you are cooking for meat-eaters, feel free to substitute vegetable stock for one made with chicken – you can't beat it for flavour and it adds a hit of protein too. I've included both my recipes in the **Building Blocks** chapter, (see pages 160–5) along with a fish-based stock (dashi) and ones that use roasted vegetables.

Of course, for days when you don't have fresh stock available, shop-bought is fine – look for pouches in the chilled cabinets. Best-quality stock cubes will work nicely, too.

In the Storecupboard

- Canned tomatoes
- Canned beans, such as chickpeas and black beans
- Stock cubes, including chicken, beef and vegetable
- Dried lentils and split peas (while pouches and cans of precooked pulses are extremely useful, I don't think they work so well in a soup, so stick to dried if at all possible)
- Tomato purée
- Canned coconut milk (full fat)
- Olive, sunflower, sesame and rapeseed oil
- Pearl barley
- Orzo and pasta shapes
- Noodles
- Brown miso paste
- Spices, including ground turmeric, coriander and cumin seeds
- Peanut butter
- Flour – plain, self-raising and strong white bread flour
- Fast-action dried yeast

In the Fridge

- Butter
- Parmesan cheese (use a vegetarian alternative, if needed)
- Cheddar cheese
- Double cream
- Yogurt
- Harissa
- Chorizo
- Pouches of stock, or chilled homemade stock
- Fresh root ginger
- Fresh herbs, including parsley, coriander, mint and dill

In the Freezer

- Edamame beans
- Prawns
- Frozen ready-chopped onions, if chopping is difficult
- Peas (no need to defrost first)
- Sweetcorn (you can use frozen kernels in cooked recipes)

Waste Not...

- Feel free to use leftovers in soup, but they generally work best if you keep them simple, rather than introducing too many flavours and ingredients.
- Many of the soups that use meat will work very nicely with some pieces of leftover cooked meat, such as chicken, turkey and beef. Soups are a great way of using up a few small pieces of meat.
- Similarly, leftover roasted vegetables, such as carrots, onions, parsnips and swede, are delicious in a soup – see the Roasted Root Vegetable Soup on page 132.
- Try to use up any leftover ingredients as quickly as possible, before their flavour and texture deteriorate.

Storing, Freezing & Reheating Soup

- Many soups will store well in the fridge for at least a couple of days and up to five. Soups that contain fresh herbs or soft leaves, such as lettuce or spinach, will not keep well at all – they will turn sludgy and lose their colour as they reheat. It can be possible to get round this by only adding soft herbs and leaves when the soup is reheated. Each recipe gives you guidance on how best to serve or store the soup.
- To store soup, cool it down as quickly as possible, and either cover or pack into airtight containers and place in the fridge. I put hot soup in non-plastic containers, such as Pyrex, stainless steel or earthenware, to allow it to cool down. Once fully cooled, I then transfer it to a plastic tub to store in the fridge.
- Some soups also freeze well, either in lidded boxes or freezerproof bags. Ensure they are packed well and labelled clearly with the date, type of soup and amount, if possible, to give an indication of how many people the batch will serve. Ensure your boxes and bags are fully sealed to prevent spoilage in the freezer. As a general rule, use soups within three months once frozen.
- To reheat, defrost fully then warm gently (do not boil!) until piping hot. If using a microwave, I like to transfer my soup to a bowl to reheat, rather than heat it in a plastic box as plastic can be harmful when heated and boxes can stain badly.

Transporting Soup

- I love to take my own food with me when I travel as I would far sooner have something I know I'll enjoy eating, rather than spending money on food I don't want to eat.
- Soup flasks have been a great investment for me. They are insulated, like an ordinary flask, but have a wider neck, which helps when pouring soups and even eating from the flask with a spoon. If I've made up a batch of soup, I reheat it in a pan and pour it into the flask using a funnel, screw on the lid and pack a spoon in my bag. I have enjoyed many soup picnics in fields, on seafront benches and in the car, either while being driven or sheltering from the weather. Either way, a delicious homemade soup offers plenty of cheer and should stay hot for at least 8 hours. Equally, a soup flask will keep chilled soups cold. Any insulated flask will do, although I have designated soup flasks, which I keep entirely separate from those I use for hot water for tea ... no one wants onion-tainted tea!
- When I was office-based, I took soup to work and reheated it in the microwave. I had a very strong, well-sealed lidded box to transport the soup in a mini cool bag, which I put in the fridge when I got to the office in the morning. If you don't have fridge access where you work, you can keep your soup cool by using an ice pack.

Tips for Serving & Presentation

- Carefully ladle or pour your soup into bowls, and don't fill them more than two-thirds full. Offer seconds, if you like, rather than over-filling the bowls. Carefully transfer them to the table, so that the soup doesn't slop around the side of the bowl. Serving your bowls on small plates can make it easier to carry them to the table as well as looking more special.
- For serving soup hot, put your bowls in a preheated oven at its lowest temperature for around 20 minutes before serving. This will keep them nice and hot without damaging the china or making them impossibly hot to touch.
- If you are keeping soup hot in a pan, keep the lid ajar to prevent any discolouration. If you are keeping soup hot in the oven, keep the door open a crack for the same reason.
- A garnish, such as a spoon of crème fraîche, a swirl of cream, oil or pesto or some whole herb leaves will add a nice visual appeal and extra flavour hit to your soup. Adding a few croutons will provide a nice contrasting texture.
- Finally, most soups in this book will feed 4–6 people (adults and older children) as a lunch or starter, but appetites do vary. Feel free to halve or double the quantities in each recipe to suit your needs.

And now, on to the recipes. I truly hope this book will show you just how brilliantly soup can offer solutions to your cooking challenges and that you will find many recipes here that will become part of your repertoire for years.

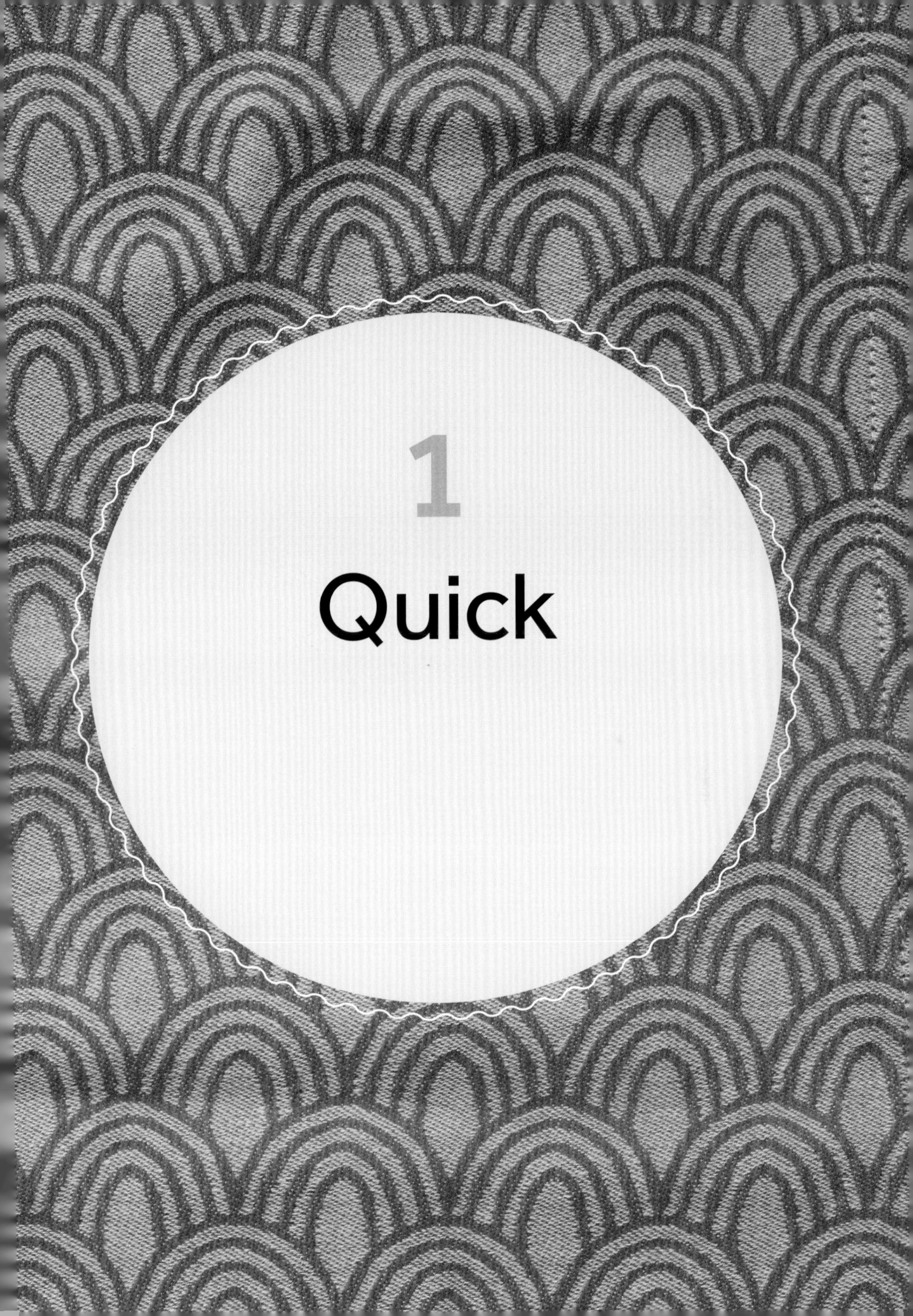

1

Quick

Thai Coconut Noodle Broth

This is a light, aromatic and creamy broth that is rich, comforting and delicately flavoured. If you can find Thai basil, do try it as it has a wonderfully unique fragrance.

SERVES 4–6

- 175g (6oz) flat rice noodles
- 400ml (14oz) can full-fat coconut milk
- 500ml (18fl oz) chicken or vegetable stock
- 1 heaped tablespoon peeled and grated fresh root ginger
- 1 fresh red chilli, finely sliced
- 1–2 tablespoons fish sauce
- 500g (1lb 2oz) cooked chicken, torn into chunks (optional)

TO SERVE

- 4 tablespoons thinly sliced spring onions
- Coriander leaves
- Handful of Thai basil leaves (optional)
- Lime wedges (optional)

1. Put the noodles in a bowl and pour over boiling water. Cover and leave for as long as the packet instructions advise. Drain and rinse immediately under cold water. You might wish to cut the noodles into shorter lengths. Set them aside to use later.
2. Put the coconut milk, stock, ginger, chilli, fish sauce and cooked chicken in a medium saucepan over a medium heat. Bring to the boil and simmer gently for around 5 minutes. Taste and adjust the seasoning, adding a little extra fish sauce if needed.
3. Divide the noodles between your serving bowls and ladle over the hot coconut broth. Serve at once, scattered with spring onions and fresh coriander. Thai basil leaves and a wedge of lime, for squeezing, make lively additions.

★ This soup is best eaten freshly made. If you are making it in advance, reheat it gently then add the herbs and toppings just before serving.

Chickpea, Tomato & Spinach Soup

If you're in need of a quick and nourishing soup, this one should fit the bill. It's so straightforward to make and is packed full of flavour.

SERVES 4–6

- 2 tablespoons olive oil, plus extra to serve
- 4 garlic cloves, finely chopped
- 400g (14oz) fresh tomatoes, chopped
- 400g (14oz) can chickpeas, drained and rinsed
- 500ml (18fl oz) vegetable stock
- 2 handfuls of fresh spinach leaves
- Salt and freshly ground pepper

1. Warm the oil in a large saucepan over a medium heat. Add the garlic and tomatoes and season with a little salt and pepper. Leave to soften over a gentle heat for around 5 minutes.
2. Add the chickpeas and stock. Simmer for around 5–10 minutes until hot. Just before serving, stir in the spinach, allowing it to wilt lightly. Taste, and add a little more seasoning if it needs it. Ladle into bowls and serve hot.

★ This soup will keep for around 5 days in the fridge and reheats well, although if you wish to prepare it in advance, don't add the spinach until you reheat the soup, just a few minutes before serving.

Hot & Sour Soup with Prawns & Noodles

I love the fragrance of this broth. It has wonderful hot, savoury and sweet notes that will give your taste buds a lift. It's also extremely easy to make, meaning you can rustle up a meal very quickly indeed.

SERVES 4

500ml (18fl oz) chicken or vegetable stock

3 tablespoons rice vinegar

2 teaspoons soy sauce

2 tablespoons granulated sugar

20g (¾oz) fresh root ginger, peeled and finely grated

1 red chilli, deseeded and finely chopped

3 spring onions, thinly sliced

200g (7oz) raw peeled prawns

100g (3½oz) cooked medium egg noodles

1. Add all the ingredients, except the prawns and noodles, to a large pan. Bring to a simmer, stirring occasionally, and add the prawns and noodles. Simmer gently for 3–5 minutes until the prawns have turned pink.
2. Taste, adjust the seasoning, adding more soy sauce if required, and serve immediately.

★ This soup is best eaten freshly made, but the base can be made in advance and stored in the fridge for up to 3 days and then reheated, adding the prawns and noodles to the hot broth for 3–5 minutes. Do not freeze this soup.

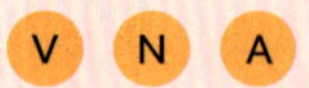

Red Lentil, Lemon & Garlic Soup

This is probably the soup I have eaten most in my life. My mum used to make something similar, and I've always enjoyed these comforting, savoury flavours. It's an incredibly simple soup, but one that is packed full of nutritious ingredients and, I think, never fails to delight.

SERVES 4–6

- 2 tablespoons olive oil
- 1 onion, chopped as finely as you can
- 2 garlic cloves, chopped
- 150g (5½oz) dried red lentils, rinsed
- 1 litre (1¾ pints) vegetable stock
- Juice of ½ lemon
- Salt and freshly ground pepper

1. Warm the oil in a large saucepan over a medium heat. Add the onion and cook for around 3 minutes until it smells fragrant and starts to turn translucent. Add the garlic and season with salt and pepper. Stir everything together well.
2. Add the lentils and stock and simmer vigorously for at least 10 minutes, until the lentils are tender. Add the lemon juice, blend, if desired, and taste. Adjust the seasoning if needed and serve immediately.

★ This soup will keep for up to 5 days in the fridge. It will also freeze very successfully – simply defrost before reheating. If the soup seems a little thick, stir through a little stock or water.

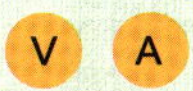

Pea & Parsley Soup

The combination of pea and parsley is perhaps less familiar than pea and mint or pea and coriander, but it's one that's really worth having up your sleeve. I always keep a bag of peas in the freezer so I can rustle this up in a hurry. I've found it's equally popular with children and adults alike.

SERVES 4–6

50g (2oz) butter or 2 tablespoons olive oil

4 spring onions, trimmed and thinly sliced

2 garlic cloves, chopped

500g (1lb 2oz) frozen peas, preferably defrosted

900ml (generous 1½ pints) hot vegetable stock

Generous handful of flat-leaf parsley, roughly chopped

Salt and freshly ground pepper

1. Melt the butter, or warm the oil, in a large saucepan over a medium heat and add the spring onions and garlic. Season with salt and pepper and gently fry for 3–4 minutes to soften the onions and garlic and release their fragrance.
2. Add the peas and cover with the hot stock. Bring to the boil and simmer for 5–8 minutes. Add the parsley and blend until smooth.
3. Taste and check the seasoning, adjusting if needed with salt and pepper. Serve immediately.

★ This soup freezes extremely well if cooled quickly. Once defrosted, reheat and serve quickly because the colour will change.

N

Miso Soup with Udon, Edamame & Salmon

This soup is wonderfully savoury in flavour yet feels clean and light to eat. The flavours are so simple; each one shines through separately.

SERVES 4

100g (3½oz) white miso paste

1 litre (1¾ pints) water

150g (5½oz) udon noodles

2–3 salmon fillets, skin and any bones removed, cut into 5cm (2in) thick slices

250g (9oz) edamame beans

TO SERVE

6 spring onions, thinly sliced

4 tablespoons toasted sesame seeds (a mix of black and white looks nice)

Soy sauce (optional)

1. Put the miso paste and water in a large saucepan and warm over a medium heat. Whisk regularly to ensure that the miso paste is evenly dispersed into the water.
2. While the miso base warms up, cook the udon noodles according to the packet instructions – they may need boiling in a separate pan. Once cooked, drain the noodles and set aside. If you wish, snip them into smaller pieces to make them easier to eat – it's up to you!
3. Once the miso is warm, add the salmon pieces and edamame and simmer for 5–10 minutes until the salmon is cooked and the edamame are warm.
4. Add the noodles, stir well and serve immediately, topped with spring onions and sesame seeds. Some people like this soup with a dash of soy sauce added at the table – again, it's up to you.

★ This soup is best eaten on the day it's made.

Foolproof Tomato Soup

I call this soup foolproof as it's very easy to make and uses canned tomatoes, so you will be able to make it at any time of the year. It is so quick to make and has a wonderful depth of flavour. For best results, use really good-quality tomatoes and balsamic vinegar.

SERVES 4–6

2 tablespoons olive oil
4 garlic cloves, chopped
2 x 400g (14oz) cans chopped tomatoes
1 teaspoon balsamic vinegar
2 teaspoons soft brown sugar
700ml (1¼ pints) vegetable stock
Salt and freshly ground pepper

1. Add the oil and garlic to a large saucepan and place over a medium heat. Gently start to cook the garlic until it is fragrant – this should just take a minute or 2.
2. Add the tomatoes, season with salt and pepper, then add the balsamic vinegar, sugar and stock. Stir well, bring to the boil then turn the heat down to simmer for 10 minutes.
3. Blend, taste and adjust the seasoning if needed. Ladle into bowls and serve hot.

★ This soup will keep very happily for up to 5 days in the fridge and reheats well. It will also freeze nicely.

N

Pasta in Brodo with Peas & Parmesan

This is inspired by a Roman recipe called pasta e piselli. As is the case with so many Italian dishes, it is deceptively simple but packed full of flavour and is sure to please diners of all ages. Brodo – Italian for broth – is often made with meat stock, so do use a chicken stock here, unless you're serving to vegetarians. This is a recipe that will welcome a spare Parmesan rind: it will impart so much flavour. Just add it to the liquid as it cooks and discard before serving.

SERVES 4–6

Bunch of spring onions, trimmed and thinly sliced
4 tablespoons olive oil
375g (13oz) frozen peas
200g (7oz) pasta
1.2 litres (2 pints) chicken stock
Parmigiano Reggiano cheese, grated, to serve, plus the rind, if you have one available

1. Put the spring onions and oil into a large saucepan. Gently cook over a medium heat until the onions smell fragrant.
2. Add the peas, pasta and stock. If you have the Parmesan rind, add it now and simmer for around 10 minutes, until the pasta is cooked.
3. Remove the rind, if using, and serve hot, with plenty of grated Parmesan on top of each bowl.

★ This soup is best eaten on the day it's made.

N

Fish Soup with Tomatoes & White Wine

This soup is light in body, yet punchy in flavour. You can use any firm white fish for this, or even salmon. This makes a fantastic lunch, starter or light dinner.

SERVES 4–6

1 tablespoon olive oil
1 onion, very thinly sliced
3 garlic cloves, chopped
400g (14oz) can chopped tomatoes
250ml (9fl oz) white wine
250ml (9fl oz) fish, chicken or vegetable stock
400g (14oz) skinless, boneless firm-fleshed fish, cut into 3cm (1¼in) chunks
Zest of ½ unwaxed lemon
Salt and freshly ground pepper
Chopped parsley, to serve (optional)

1. Warm the oil in a large saucepan. Add the onion and cook for around 5 minutes until it starts to soften. Add the garlic and tomatoes and season well with salt and pepper. Stir and simmer for a further 5 minutes.
2. Add the wine, stock and fish, bring to a simmer and cook on a gentle heat for around 10 minutes until the fish is fully cooked. Add the lemon zest, taste and adjust the seasoning adding more salt and pepper if it needs it.
3. Ladle into bowls and serve immediately, garnished with a little chopped fresh parsley, if you wish.

★ This soup is best eaten on the day it's made.

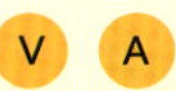

Sweetcorn Chowder

This is another recipe that's so popular with people of all ages. The sweetcorn adds a wonderful texture and pleasing pop of sweetness, which balances well with the more savoury soup base. If you can't get hold of fresh corn, I think frozen works extremely well – I keep a bag in the freezer to use in soups.

SERVES 4–6

25g (1oz) butter or 2 tablespoons olive or rapeseed oil

6 spring onions, trimmed and thinly sliced

300g (10½oz) sweetcorn kernels, ideally fresh, or use frozen

1 floury potato, peeled and finely chopped

500ml (18fl oz) hot vegetable stock

300ml (10fl oz) milk

Salt and freshly ground pepper

1. Melt the butter, or warm the oil, in a large saucepan over a low heat. Add the spring onion and cook until softened but not coloured. This will take around 5 minutes.
2. Add the sweetcorn and potato and season with salt and pepper. Stir well and add the stock and milk. Put a lid on and simmer gently for around 15 minutes or until the potato is cooked.
3. Blend, then taste to check if it needs extra seasoning. Ladle into bowls and serve immediately.

★ This soup will keep for 5 days in the fridge or can be successfully frozen, defrosted and reheated.

2 No-Cook

Creamy Pea Soup

This is such an easy soup to make and a brilliant way to use leftover cooked peas; in fact, it's often worth cooking extra if you're planning on making this soup. You can, though, use defrosted ones. A high-speed blender is particularly useful here to get a super-smooth result, especially if you're using defrosted peas.

SERVES 4–6

- 600g (1lb 5oz) frozen peas, either defrosted or cooked and cooled
- 600ml (20fl oz) vegetable stock
- ½ spring onion, trimmed and thinly sliced
- 4 tablespoons double cream, plus extra to serve
- Salt

1. This couldn't be much easier – simply put all the ingredients into a blender and whizz until smooth. Taste, add more salt or cream if it needs it.
2. Transfer the soup to a jug, cover with clingfilm and chill for at least 20 minutes and up to 2 hours before serving with an extra swirl of cream.

★ This soup will keep for up to 2 days in the fridge – you might just need to stir it before serving as sometimes it can separate a little. This isn't, though, a soup to freeze.

Gazpacho

On a really hot day, gazpacho is the perfect meal or starter. The secret is getting the balance right between the flavour of the vegetables, oil and vinegar. You might like to keep back some of the vegetables to create an attractive garnish for the soup bowls. This is optional, so do feel free to blend all of the vegetables together.

SERVES 4–6

½ large cucumber, peeled and roughly chopped

2 large red peppers, deseeded and roughly chopped

6 large, ripe tomatoes, cored and roughly chopped

2 shallots, roughly chopped

3 garlic cloves, chopped

100g (3½oz) best-quality bread, such as sourdough, roughly torn into pieces

3 tbsp extra virgin olive oil

2 tablespoons sherry vinegar

Salt

1. Blend the cucumber, peppers, tomatoes and shallots to a rough purée in a food processor, reserving, if you wish, a couple of chunks of each vegetable as a garnish.
2. Add the garlic, bread, olive oil and sherry vinegar to the food processor and blend again until the consistency is to your liking – either textured or perfectly smooth. Taste and add salt if it needs it.
3. Transfer the soup to a jug, cover with clingfilm and chill for at least 20 minutes and up to 2 hours.
4. Cut any reserved vegetables into small cubes. When ready to serve, ladle the gazpacho into bowls and garnish with the cubed vegetables.

Ajo Blanco

This is a fantastic chilled soup that traces its roots to southern Spain during its Moorish past. It's wonderfully refreshing and light in hot weather. The quality of the ingredients does make a difference to the end result so try to use really good-quality bread, oil and vinegar. Try adding one, some or all of the suggested toppings for a final flourish.

SERVES 4–6 AS A STARTER

1 slice (40–50g/1½–1¾oz) stale, good-quality white bread – baguette or ciabatta is ideal

100g (3½oz) blanched almonds

1 garlic clove

50ml (2fl oz) extra virgin olive oil, plus extra to serve

1 teaspoon sherry vinegar

250ml (9fl oz) water

Pinch of salt

TO SERVE

Finely diced cucumber

Toasted flaked almonds

Sliced grapes (optional)

Finely diced apple (optional)

1. Simply add all the ingredients to a blender and whizz until smooth. Taste and adjust the seasoning adding more salt if it needs it.
2. Transfer the soup to a jug, cover with clingfilm and chill for at least 20 minutes and up to 2 hours or, if you're in a hurry, add an ice cube or 2 to each bowl.
3. Top with the cucumber and almonds. If you decide you'd like a bit more sweetness, add some grapes or apple as you serve.

★ This soup is best eaten freshly made.

Chilled Cucumber & Tahini Soup

This soup has a light and refreshing texture and a wonderfully savoury flavour. It should really satisfy the tastebuds in warm weather.

SERVES 4

700g (1lb 9oz) cucumber, cut into 1cm (½in) cubes

100g (3½oz) tahini

4 garlic cloves

4 tablespoons fresh lemon juice

2 teaspoons salt

1. Add all the ingredients to a blender and whizz until smooth – it will froth a little. Transfer the soup to a jug, cover with clingfilm and chill for at least 20 minutes and up to 2 hours.
2. Taste, add more salt if it needs it, then serve ice cold.

V

Chilled Watercress Soup

Here is another incredibly simple soup to make – ideal for a starter or light lunch for any watercress-lover, as its punchy flavour really comes through when eaten raw. A high-speed blender is particularly useful to get a super-smooth result when making this soup, as the watercress does take time to break down. You can make it using a stick blender, but keep an eye on the blades as the watercress can tangle a little while it's being blended.

SERVES 4–6

160g (5¾oz) fresh watercress
500ml (18fl oz) vegetable stock
50ml (2fl oz) double cream
Salt

1. Simply add all the ingredients to a high-speed blender and whizz until smooth. Transfer the soup to a jug, cover with clingfilm and chill for at least 20 minutes and up to 2 hours.
2. Taste, add more salt or cream if it needs it, and serve chilled.

★ This soup is best served soon after making; it is not one to prepare in advance as the watercress will deteriorate quickly.

Ajo Blanco

This is a fantastic chilled soup that traces its roots to southern Spain during its Moorish past. It's wonderfully refreshing and light in hot weather. The quality of the ingredients does make a difference to the end result so try to use really good-quality bread, oil and vinegar. Try adding one, some or all of the suggested toppings for a final flourish.

SERVES 4–6 AS A STARTER

1 slice (40–50g/1½–1¾oz) stale, good-quality white bread – baguette or ciabatta is ideal

100g (3½oz) blanched almonds

1 garlic clove

50ml (2fl oz) extra virgin olive oil, plus extra to serve

1 teaspoon sherry vinegar

250ml (9fl oz) water

Pinch of salt

TO SERVE

Finely diced cucumber

Toasted flaked almonds

Sliced grapes (optional)

Finely diced apple (optional)

1. Simply add all the ingredients to a blender and whizz until smooth. Taste and adjust the seasoning adding more salt if it needs it.
2. Transfer the soup to a jug, cover with clingfilm and chill for at least 20 minutes and up to 2 hours or, if you're in a hurry, add an ice cube or 2 to each bowl.
3. Top with the cucumber and almonds. If you decide you'd like a bit more sweetness, add some grapes or apple as you serve.

★ This soup is best eaten freshly made.

Hiyajiru

This is a Japanese chilled soup made with miso, dashi (fish stock) and other traditional seasonings. Texture is added with tofu, sliced cucumber and seaweed. It's such an easy recipe to rustle up and the ingredients can usually be found in larger supermarkets or specialist stores and definitely online. *There's a recipe for making your own dashi on page 162.*

SERVES 4–6

25g (1oz) red miso

20ml (¾fl oz) toasted sesame oil

25ml (1fl oz) Japanese rice vinegar

1 tablespoon mirin

300ml (10fl oz) dashi

300g (10½oz) silken tofu, drained and cut into 1–2cm (½–¾in) cubes

¼ cucumber, thinly sliced

20g (¾oz) ready-to-eat wakame seaweed salad

Ice cubes, to serve (optional)

1. Put the miso, sesame oil, vinegar and mirin in a large jug and whisk together. Add the dashi and whisk again. Chill for at least an hour before serving.
2. To serve, divide the chunks of tofu between bowls. Add the cucumber and seaweed and pour the chilled liquid over the top. Add some ice cubes, if you wish, and serve straight away.

★ This soup is best eaten freshly made. You can keep the liquid base for up to 2 days in the fridge if needed, then add the tofu, cucumber and seaweed just before serving. This is not a soup to freeze.

V

Chilled Watermelon, Cucumber & Lime Soup

Watermelon is so refreshing and hydrating and it makes a fantastic chilled soup. This combination is a really interesting one, and doesn't taste quite as sweet as you might expect.

SERVES 4–6

650g (1lb 7oz) prepared watermelon, rind and seeds removed

200g (7oz) cucumber, peeled and chopped

½ banana shallot, chopped

Squeeze of lime juice

Salt

1. As with so many chilled soups, all you need to do here is blend the ingredients together until smooth. Transfer the soup to a jug, cover with clingfilm and chill for at least 20 minutes and up to 2 hours.
2. Taste, add more salt and/or lime juice if it needs it, and chill until you wish to serve.

★ This soup is best eaten freshly made; it is not one to prepare in advance, store or freeze.

Levantine-Inspired Chilled Yogurt & Cucumber Soup

I've enjoyed some fantastic cold soups from the Levant, and this is my attempt to recreate something similar.

SERVES 4–6

400g (14oz) cucumber, peeled and chopped, reserving some for a garnish

½ banana shallot, chopped

1 small garlic clove, chopped

4 mint leaves

200ml (7fl oz) yogurt

Salt

1. Simply add all the ingredients to a high-speed blender and whizz until smooth. Taste, and add more salt if it needs it.
2. Transfer the soup to a jug, cover with clingfilm and chill for at least 20 minutes and up to 2 hours. Serve ice cold scattered with the reserved cucumber.

3 Budget

Creamy Potato Soup

This is a simple, time-honoured recipe, and it's wonderfully tasty and satisfying. I am especially fond of this soup served with a big swirl of parsley pesto.

SERVES 6

50g (2oz) butter

1 large leek, trimmed and thinly sliced

2 garlic cloves, chopped

500g (1lb 2oz) floury potatoes, cut into 1cm (½in) cubes

800ml (scant 1½ pints) vegetable stock

100ml (3½fl oz) milk or double cream

Salt and lots of freshly ground pepper

Parsley Pesto (see page 140), to serve (optional)

1. Melt the butter in a large, heavy saucepan over a low heat. Add the leek and garlic. Season with salt and pepper and allow to soften for 15 minutes.
2. Add the potatoes and stock and cook for around 20 minutes until the potatoes are just tender.
3. Add the milk, or cream, and blend the soup until smooth. Taste and adjust the seasoning before serving with some pesto, if you like.

★ This soup will keep for up to 5 days in the fridge, and freezes well.

Lettuce & Spring Onion Soup

This one is a wonderfully light soup with a delicate and savoury flavour. It's a great way of making a sophisticated meal out of very few ingredients. I think it's particularly good as a starter or for lunch.

SERVES 4–6

25g (1oz) butter

6 spring onions, trimmed and thinly sliced

2 Cos or Romaine lettuces, chopped

1 litre (1¾ pints) vegetable stock

Salt and freshly ground pepper

1. Melt the butter in a large saucepan over a medium heat. Add the spring onions, season with a little salt and pepper and soften them over a gentle heat for around 2 minutes.
2. Next, add the lettuce, stir and fry for another couple of minutes before adding the stock. Simmer for around 10 minutes until the ingredients have softened nicely.
3. Blend, taste and add a little more seasoning if it needs it. Serve hot, ladled into bowls.

★ This soup is best eaten freshly made and is not one to store or freeze.

Green Lentil, Garlic & Mint Soup

I've eaten soups similar to this one in both Spain and Turkey and absolutely love the depth of flavour from such simple, affordable ingredients. I prefer the texture when the soup is partially blended. Serve with my garlic yogurt, or with Greek yogurt.

SERVES 4

300g (10½oz) dried green lentils

3 onions, thinly sliced

3 tablespoons olive oil, plus extra for drizzling

4 garlic cloves, finely sliced

1 teaspoon ground cumin

1.7 litres (3 pints) cold water

Juice of ½ lemon, plus extra to taste

Good handful of fresh mint leaves, roughly chopped, plus extra to serve

Salt

1–2 tablespoons Garlic Yogurt (see page 144), to serve

1. Rinse the lentils well in cold water and leave to drain in a colander.
2. Put the onions and oil into a large, lidded saucepan over a medium heat and sauté for around 10 minutes until softened. Season with salt. Add the garlic and sauté for another 1–2 minutes.
3. Now, add the cumin, lentils and water. Bring to the boil and simmer with the lid on until the lentils are tender. This should take around 30–40 minutes.
4. Once the lentils are tender, squeeze in the lemon juice and taste. The soup might need more lemon juice and salt, too. Stir in the chopped mint at the very last minute. When the soup tastes to your liking, it's ready. I like to half-blend it using a stick blender, so that the texture is a pleasing mix of smooth and chunky.
5. Serve in bowls with a swirl of the garlic yogurt, an extra drizzle of oil and some chopped mint on top.

★ The soup will keep well for up to 5 days in the fridge, but ensure the toppings are stored separately. Do not freeze this soup.

Swede & Ginger Soup

Swede is a bit of an unsung hero but it's a brilliant ingredient for soup, and the combination of swede and ginger is wonderfully vibrant and warming. Blending this soup gives it a fantastically rich and creamy texture.

SERVES 6

2 tablespoons olive oil
1 onion, thinly sliced
2 potatoes, diced
1 swede, peeled and diced (you want about 750g/1lb 10oz prepared weight)
1.4 litres (2½ pints) vegetable stock
1–2 tablespoons peeled and grated or finely chopped fresh root ginger
Salt and freshly ground pepper

1. Warm the oil in a large, lidded saucepan over a medium heat. Add the onion, season with salt and cook over a medium–high heat for around 10 minutes, or until it softens.
2. Add the potatoes, swede and stock and season with pepper. Simmer for around 20 minutes with the lid on, then add the ginger and simmer for a further 20 minutes or so, until all the vegetables are tender.
3. Blend until smooth, taste and adjust the seasoning if it needs it, and serve straight away.

★ This soup will keep well for up to 5 days in the fridge and it freezes nicely, too.

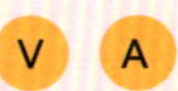

Celery & Leek Soup

This is a simple, traditional and comforting soup that is full of flavour. Celery and leek are classic ingredients to make both soups and stocks, and for good reason: they are inexpensive, widely available and the result is quite delicious – you'll be batch-making this for your freezer.

SERVES 4–6

2 tablespoons olive oil
1 leek, trimmed and sliced
4 celery sticks, trimmed and sliced
2 garlic cloves, chopped
2 floury potatoes, chopped
2 bay leaves
1 litre (1¾ pints) vegetable stock
100ml (3½fl oz) milk (optional)
Salt and freshly ground pepper

1. Warm the oil in a large saucepan over a medium heat. Add the leek, celery and garlic, season with salt and pepper and cook for around 10 minutes until the leek has started to soften.
2. Add the potatoes, bay leaves and stock and bring to the boil, then reduce the heat and simmer with a lid on for around 30 minutes or until all the vegetables are tender.
3. Blend the soup and add the milk if you wish, then taste and adjust the seasoning adding salt and pepper if needed. Serve immediately.

★ This soup will keep for up to 5 days in the fridge and freezes well.

Lemon Orzo Soup

This soup could hardly be easier to make and uses very inexpensive ingredients. I've found it to be a favourite of everyone, young and old. Serve just as it is or, for meat-eaters, once the pasta is cooked, I like to add a handful or two of cooked chicken or turkey to the broth for a protein boost.

SERVES 4–6

1 tablespoon olive oil
2 onions, chopped
80g (2¾oz) orzo
Zest of 2 unwaxed lemons
1 litre (1¾ pints) vegetable stock
1–2 handfuls of cooked chicken or turkey, skin and bones removed (optional)
Parmigiano Reggiano, grated, to serve (optional)

1. Warm the oil in a large saucepan over a medium heat. Add the onions, season with a little salt and pepper and soften them over a gentle heat for around 10 minutes.
2. Add the orzo, lemon zest and stock and simmer for 10–15 minutes until the orzo is tender. If you're adding cooked chicken or turkey, put it into the broth now.
3. Ladle the soup into bowls, top with some grated Parmigiano Reggiano if you fancy it, and serve immediately.

★ This soup will keep for around 5 days in the fridge and will reheat well. Do not freeze this soup.

Carrot & Coriander Seed Soup

This vegetable soup is wonderfully fragrant, simple and delicious. It's one I often make when I don't have many fresh ingredients to hand – I can usually rustle up an onion and a handful of carrots. The coriander seeds will happily stay in the storecupboard for months. This recipe scales up very well if needed.

SERVES 4

1 tablespoon olive oil
1 large onion, chopped
450g (1lb) carrots, chopped
1 heaped teaspoon whole coriander seeds
1.2 litres (2 pints) vegetable stock
Squeeze of lemon juice
Salt and freshly ground pepper

1. Warm the oil in a large saucepan over a medium heat. Add the onion, carrots and coriander seeds, season with salt and pepper and cook over a medium heat for around 10 minutes until fragrant and softened a little.
2. Add the stock and bring to the boil, then reduce the heat and simmer with a lid on for around 20 minutes or until the carrots are really tender.
3. Blend the soup then add the lemon juice, taste and season with extra salt and pepper if needed.
4. Serve immediately – or keep for up to 5 days in the fridge for reheating on demand. It also freezes well.

N

Polentina

This is a fantastic, Italian-inspired soup made using instant polenta, which is made from ground maize, and some good stock. It's quick to prepare, nourishing and flavourful. It does, though, need to be eaten quickly once it's made. It thickens as it cools and its texture becomes dense and slightly gelatinous. For an extra layer of flavour and crunch, serve your polentina topped with some peppery leaves and my Crispy Bacon Sprinkle. If you find you have any leftover polentina, do as the Italians do: transfer it to a baking tray or loaf tin, spread it out into a smooth layer then chill it in the fridge. Once cold, it can be cut into cubes, fried in a little oil and served as a snack – delicious!

SERVES 4–6

- 1.2 litres (2 pints) chicken or vegetable stock
- 150g (5½oz) instant polenta
- 4 tablespoons extra virgin olive oil
- 25g (1oz) butter
- Salt and freshly ground pepper

TO SERVE

- 100g (3½oz) Parmesan cheese, grated
- Handful of watercress leaves or chopped kale
- Crispy Bacon Sprinkle (see page 143)

1. Bring the stock to a simmer in a large saucepan over a medium heat. Once simmering, add the polenta, season with salt and pepper and whisk frequently for 10–15 minutes. Keep the temperature medium so that the polenta cooks gently. The soup will thicken quickly.
2. Stir in the oil and butter and taste. Add more salt and pepper if you like.
3. As soon as the polenta is smooth, the soup is ready to serve. Ladle into bowls and top generously with Parmesan, along with some watercress or kale leaves and some of the crispy bacon, if desired. Serve and eat straight away – this soup won't wait for long.

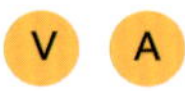

Roasted Parsnip & Harissa Soup

I particularly love the combination here because the sweetness of parsnips and earthy spice notes of harissa work so well together. I often make this soup with rose or smoked chilli harissa. Brands do vary in terms of heat and some can be surprisingly punchy, so if you are unsure how spicy yours is, try adding less to start with and building the heat if you want to.

SERVES 4–6

- 1 onion, cut into wedges
- 500g (1lb 2oz) parsnips, cut into 2cm (¾in) chunks
- 1 tablespoon olive oil
- 1 litre (1¾ pints) vegetable stock
- 1–2 tablespoons harissa, to taste
- Salt and freshly ground pepper

1. Preheat the oven to 180°C/160°C fan (350°F), Gas Mark 4.
2. Put the onion wedges and parsnip chunks into an ovenproof dish, drizzle with olive oil, season with salt and pepper and roast for around 40 minutes, turning the vegetables halfway through to ensure they cook evenly, until tender and lightly browned.
3. Transfer the roasted vegetables to a large saucepan and pour in the stock. Bring to a simmer over a medium heat and cook for around 10 minutes.
4. Blend the soup until smooth then stir in the harissa, a little at a time, and taste to build up the flavour and heat intensity so that you can judge the level of spiciness for your taste. Check the seasoning and serve immediately.

★ This soup can be stored for up to 5 days in the fridge, or frozen if you wish to make it in advance.

Cuban-Inspired Black Bean Soup

This is a richly flavoured, thick and creamy soup that's based on one that's eaten a lot in Havana and the western provinces of Cuba. It's pleasingly filling and makes for a satisfying meal in a bowl. This recipe works particularly well with a few toppings to add contrasting flavours and textures – I've suggested some that I like to pair it with.

SERVES 4–6

1 tablespoon sunflower or rapeseed oil

2 onions, finely chopped

6 garlic cloves, chopped

1 large red pepper, deseeded and chopped

1 heaped teaspoon whole cumin seeds

1 heaped teaspoon dried oregano

1 teaspoon salt

Freshly ground pepper

3 bay leaves

2 x 400g (14oz) cans black beans, drained and rinsed

500ml (18fl oz) vegetable stock

TOPPINGS (OPTIONAL)

Crushed tortilla chips

Soured cream

Sliced red onion or avocado

Chopped fresh coriander

1. Warm the oil in a large saucepan over a medium heat. Add the onions and fry for around 5 minutes until they start to soften. Add the garlic, red pepper, cumin, oregano, salt, pepper and bay leaves and fry for another 5 minutes.
2. Add the beans and stock and simmer for 15–20 minutes until the beans and vegetables are tender.
3. Blend lightly, to achieve a smoother consistency, but still with some texture. Taste, adjust the seasoning if needed and serve immediately, with any of the toppings you fancy.

★ This soup is best eaten freshly made. If you need to make it in advance, don't add the toppings before serving.

Red Pepper & Butter Bean Soup

Red peppers are extremely popular in soups – everyone enjoys their sweetness and tang – while butter beans lend body and creaminess, so this one is sure to be a crowd-pleaser.

SERVES 4–6

2 tablespoons olive oil, plus extra for drizzling
2 onions, chopped
4 garlic cloves, chopped
2 red peppers, deseeded and chopped
3 large fresh tomatoes, cored and chopped
2 x 400g (14oz) can butter beans, drained and rinsed
750ml (generous 1¼ pints) vegetable stock
1–2 tablespoons lemon juice
Salt and freshly ground pepper

1. Warm the oil in a large saucepan over a medium heat. Add the onions, garlic and red peppers, season with salt and pepper and cook for around 10 minutes until the onions have softened a little.
2. Add the tomatoes, butter beans and stock and bring to the boil, then reduce the heat and simmer with a lid on for around 20 minutes, or until the onions and peppers are tender.
3. Blend the soup then add the lemon juice, taste and season with extra salt and pepper if needed. Serve immediately, drizzled with a little extra olive oil, if you like.

★ This soup will keep for up to 5 days in the fridge and freezes well.

Onion, Apple & Thyme Soup

This soup is wonderfully decadent with a pleasing sweet–savoury flavour. The onions and apples make up the bulk of the soup and are very economical ingredients. A little dash of cream adds a pleasing richness. This soup is a very nice option to serve for a lunch or as a starter. Some Homemade Croutons or Fougasse make a fantastic accompaniment.

SERVES 4–6

50g (2oz) butter or 2 tablespoons olive oil

3 onions, chopped

3 large eating apples, peeled and chopped

1 tablespoon fresh thyme leaves, or 1½ teaspoons dried

1 teaspoon Dijon mustard

700ml (1¼ pints) vegetable stock

2 tablespoons double cream (more, if preferred)

Salt and freshly ground pepper

TO SERVE (OPTIONAL)

Homemade Croutons (see page 157) or Fougasse (see page 148)

1. Melt the butter or, warm the oil, in a large saucepan over a medium heat. Add the onions and apples and fry for around 10 minutes until they start to soften.
2. Season with thyme, salt and pepper and stir well. Add the mustard and stock and simmer for around 20 minutes until the onions and apples are tender. Add the cream.
3. Blend until smooth then taste and check the seasoning – it may need a little more salt and pepper. Serve immediately, with Homemade Croutons or Fougasse.

★ This soup will keep for up to 5 days in the fridge. It also freezes and reheats extremely well.

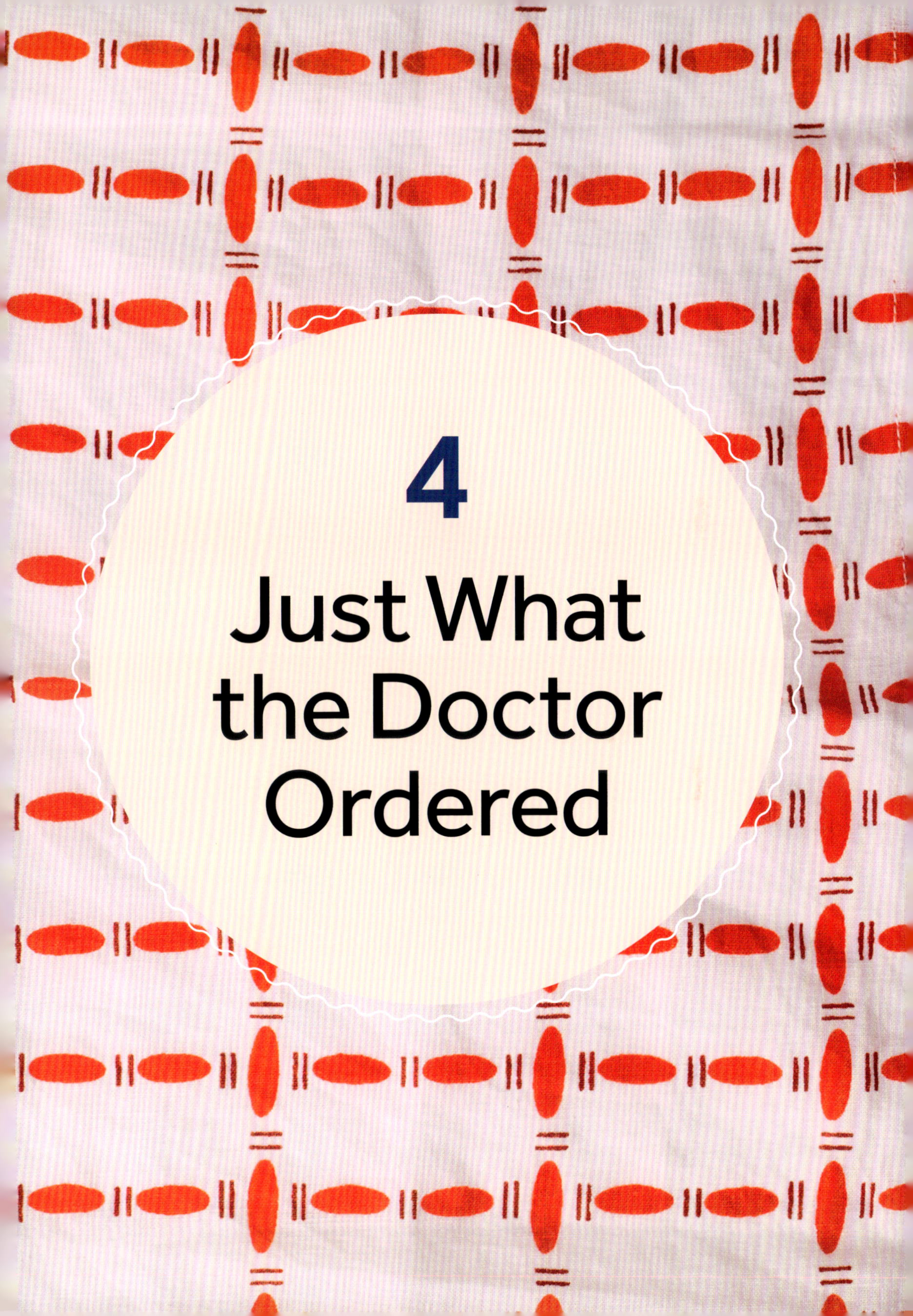

4

Just What the Doctor Ordered

10-Vegetable Soup

As its name suggests, this soup is packed full of fresh vegetables, which instinctively I feel must do a lot of good. Current research indicates that increasing both the amount and diversity of vegetables and other plants in our diet can offer significant benefits to long-term health as they are rich in fibre, vitamins and minerals. This soup is so full of flavour and I've found it's very popular with children and adults alike.

SERVES 4–6

2 tablespoons good-quality olive oil

1 onion, finely chopped

3 garlic cloves, finely chopped

1 leek, trimmed and thinly sliced

1 carrot, cut into 1cm (½in) dice

1 celery stick, trimmed and chopped

½ fennel bulb, thinly sliced

1 red or orange pepper, deseeded and cut into 1cm (½in) dice

200g (7oz) squash, peeled and cut into 1cm (½in) chunks

400g (14oz) can chopped tomatoes

500ml (18fl oz) hot vegetable stock

100g (3½oz) kale leaves or spring greens, stripped from the stalk and chopped into small pieces

Salt and freshly ground pepper

1. Warm the oil in a large saucepan over a medium heat. Add the onion, garlic and leek and allow to cook for around 10 minutes until softened.
2. Season and add the carrot, celery, fennel, pepper and squash and cook for a further 5 minutes, stirring continuously. Add the tomatoes and stir well.
3. Next, add the hot stock. Stir and allow to simmer for 45 minutes until the vegetables are fully tender.
4. Stir in the kale or greens, allow 5 minutes for them to wilt in the hot liquid. Taste to check the seasoning, adding a little more salt or pepper if it needs it, then remove from the heat and serve immediately.

★ This soup will keep for up to 5 days in the fridge and also freezes well. If you are preparing it in advance, it's best not to add the kale until you reheat the soup to ensure they don't overcook and turn sludgy.

Get Better Soon Chicken Soup

This is a thoroughly delicious chicken and vegetable soup, one that's a wonderful addition to your repertoire for good times and bad. Different cultures around the world revere chicken soup for its health-giving properties, and it's an important pillar of many families' food traditions both to maintain and improve their health. This is my version and it is packed full of vegetables and flavour – it's so tasty that some of my recipe testers voted it their favourite recipe in the book.

SERVES 4–6

1 tablespoon olive oil or butter
2 onions, sliced
1 leek, trimmed and sliced
2 carrots, chopped
2 celery sticks, trimmed and sliced
1 garlic clove, chopped
300g (10½oz) cooked chicken
2 bay leaves
1 litre (1¾ pints) chicken stock
50–100ml (2–3½fl oz) double cream (optional)
Salt and freshly ground pepper

1. Warm the oil, or melt the butter, in a large saucepan over a medium heat. Add the onions, leek, carrots, celery and garlic and season with salt and pepper. Soften for around 15 minutes until the vegetables have started to cook down and become tender. Stir, turning them frequently, so that they don't catch on the base or colour too much.
2. Next, add the chicken, bay leaves and stock and simmer for 30–60 minutes to extract all the flavour from the meat.
3. Serve the soup as it is or blend it first. I like to half blend it so that it is creamier in texture, but retains some chunks. The cream is optional, but adds a lovely richness, so stir in a little or more as you wish, just before serving. Either way, make sure you taste the soup to check the seasoning and add salt and pepper to boost the flavour before serving.

★ This soup will keep for up to 5 days in the fridge, although it is not one to freeze.

Kale, White Bean & Lemon Broth

This is a vibrant and clean-tasting soup that I find very uplifting to eat because it makes me feel I'm doing myself some good. The light broth is nutrient-rich and the beans, kale and garlic add fibre, vitamins and minerals. I like to serve it with a good drizzle of olive oil and sometimes a grating of Parmigiano Reggiano. The Fougasse or Focaccia (see pages 148 and 151) are wonderful accompaniments.

SERVES 4–6

- 2 tablespoons olive oil, plus extra to serve
- 1 large onion, thinly sliced
- 2 celery sticks, thinly sliced
- 4 garlic cloves, finely chopped
- 1 tablespoon finely chopped rosemary needles
- 400g (14oz) can white beans, such as cannellini or haricot, drained and rinsed
- 1 litre (1¾ pints) vegetable or chicken stock
- 250g (9oz) kale leaves, stripped from the stalks and roughly chopped
- 1 tablespoon lemon juice
- Salt and freshly ground pepper
- Grated Parmigiano Reggiano cheese, to serve

1. Warm the oil in a large saucepan over a medium heat. Add the onions and celery, season with a little salt and pepper and soften them for around 10 minutes, adjusting the heat so that they don't catch on the base or colour too much. Next, add the garlic, rosemary and beans. Stir and fry for another couple of minutes.
2. Stir in the stock and simmer for around 15–20 minutes until the ingredients have melded nicely and the beans and onions are tender. Add the kale and simmer for a further 5 minutes until it is tender.
3. Stir in the lemon juice, taste and add a little more salt or juice if it needs it. Ladle into bowls and top with a drizzle of oil, and some Parmigiano Reggiano, and enjoy nice and hot.

★ This soup will keep for around 2 days in the fridge and will reheat well, although if you wish to prepare this in advance, don't add the kale until you reheat the soup a few minutes before serving.

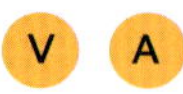

Red Lentil, Turmeric & Lemon Soup

The combination of lentils, turmeric and lemon is truly special, and this is a soup I make often at home. This is a simple and highly nutritious soup. Red lentils are full of fibre, complex carbohydrates and protein. Turmeric is great for giving a boost to the immune system, and it tastes absolutely delicious. I think this soup works wonderfully well served with a generous sprinkle of the Toasted Seed Mix (see page 144.)

SERVES 6

3 large onions, chopped
3 tablespoons olive oil
1 teaspoon ground turmeric
350g (12oz) dried red lentils, rinsed
1.5 litres (2¾ pints) vegetable stock
1–2 teaspoons freshly squeezed lemon juice
Toasted Seed Mix (See page 144), to serve (optional)
Salt and freshly ground pepper

1. Put the onion and oil into a large saucepan over a gentle heat and allow the onion to soften but not colour.
2. Next, add the turmeric and cook for a minute or 2, then add the lentils. Season generously with salt and pepper, then add the stock. Bring to the boil and simmer for around 10–20 minutes until the lentils are soft.
3. Whizz the soup until reasonably smooth. Taste and add a teaspoon of lemon juice before tasting again and add more juice or adjust the seasoning if needed. Serve straight away with a sprinkle of Toasted Seed Mix if liked.

★ This soup will keep for up to 5 days in the fridge. It reheats well, but you might find it needs a dash of water to thin it a touch. This soup also freezes well.

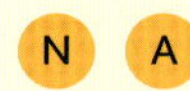

Chicken & Sweetcorn Soup

This is a wonderfully warming soup and packed with flavour. For me, this is pure comfort food as it is immensely soothing and cheering. I like to serve it with some cream for richness, but you don't have to. This is one of the few recipes in the book that does need some time to simmer, but the preparation couldn't be much easier.

SERVES 4–6

75g (2¾oz) butter or 3 tablespoons olive oil

500g (1lb 2oz) sweetcorn kernels, fresh or frozen

300g (10½oz) floury potatoes, diced

2 bay leaves

1–2 chicken legs, skin removed

1 litre (1¾ pints) chicken stock, plus extra as needed

150ml (5fl oz) double cream (optional)

Salt and freshly ground pepper

1. Melt the butter, or warm the oil, in a large, lidded saucepan over a medium heat. Add the sweetcorn kernels, potatoes, bay leaves and chicken legs. Season with salt and pepper and stir well. Add the stock, stir again then put the lid on. Simmer for at least an hour over a low–medium heat until the chicken is really tender.
2. Remove the chicken legs, strip the meat from the bones and add it back to the pan. Remove the bay leaves and stir in the cream, if using (if you are not using cream you may want to add more stock). Taste the soup, adding more salt and pepper if needed.
3. Serve the soup as it is or blend it, partially or fully, depending on how you prefer the texture. I like to partially blend it using a stick blender, which breaks up the potato chunks and thickens the soup somewhat. Serve hot.

★ This soup will keep for up to 5 days in the fridge. Be sure to reheat it over a gentle heat so that there is no risk of the cream splitting. Do not freeze this soup.

Carrot, Ginger & Orange Soup

The combination of carrots with fresh ginger and orange is just wonderful. This is a soup to make when you fancy a burst of lively flavours on the palate. What's even better is that the fresh ginger and orange both provide a range of vitamins and are anti-inflammatory, which is good for digestion. Add as much or as little ginger as you prefer.

SERVES 4–6

2 tablespoons olive or rapeseed oil

1 large onion, chopped

20–50g (¾–2oz) piece of fresh root ginger, peeled and chopped

400g (14oz) carrots, chopped

1 litre (1¾ pints) vegetable stock

4 tablespoons fresh orange juice

Salt and freshly ground pepper

1. Warm the oil in a large saucepan over a gentle heat. Add the onion and leave to soften but not colour. Add the ginger and carrots and cook for another couple of minutes. Season generously with salt and pepper. Add the stock, bring to the boil and simmer for around 10–20 minutes until the carrots are soft.
2. Add the orange juice and blend the soup until smooth and silky. Taste, adjust the seasoning if it needs it, and serve straight away.

★ This soup will keep for up to 5 days in the fridge and will freeze and reheat successfully.

Spring Greens Broth

This is another broth that feels like it's really doing me some good every time I eat it. Spring greens – like all green, leafy vegetables – are rich in iron, vitamins and minerals and antioxidants, and this is a great way of boosting your green vegetable intake. You can vary the greens you use, depending on what is available. Any sort of green cabbage or leaves can work: kale, chard, hispi or Savoy cabbage – even sprout tops – are all great options. Parsley makes a pleasing alternative to dill, if needed.

SERVES 4–6

2 tablespoons olive oil, plus extra to serve

1 leek, trimmed and thinly sliced

2 celery sticks, thinly sliced

4 garlic cloves, finely chopped

400g (14oz) can cannellini beans, drained and rinsed

1 litre (1¾ pints) vegetable stock

250g (9oz) spring greens or chard, leaves stripped from the stalks and roughly chopped

1 tablespoon lemon juice

10g (¼oz) fresh dill fronds, picked from the stalks

Salt and freshly ground pepper

1. Warm the oil in a large saucepan over a medium heat. Add the leek and celery, season with salt and pepper and cook for around 10 minutes.
2. Add the garlic and beans. Fry, stirring, for another couple of minutes, then add the stock and simmer for around 10 minutes until the vegetables are tender.
3. Add the spring greens, or chard, and simmer for a further 5 minutes until they are slightly wilted. Stir in the lemon juice and dill, taste and add a little more salt or lemon if it needs it. Ladle into bowls and serve hot.

★ This soup will keep for around 2 days in the fridge and will reheat well, although if you wish to prepare this in advance, don't add either the greens or the dill until you reheat the soup a few minutes before serving.

Beef, Pearl Barley & Tomato Soup

This is a simple, traditional soup that has a wonderful rich, meaty flavour. The pearl barley turns this into a hearty soup, not too dissimilar to a stew. It is the sort of meal that has fortified and sustained people for generations. Barley is rich in antioxidants and fibre, while beef provides plenty of protein and iron – use either thinly sliced steak or some leftover roasted meat.

SERVES 4–6

1 tablespoon olive or rapeseed oil

1 onion, chopped

2 celery sticks, trimmed and chopped

1 carrot, chopped

250g (9oz) raw beef steak or use cooked leftovers from a roast, thinly sliced

400g (14oz) can chopped tomatoes

60g (2¼oz) pearl barley

1 litre (1¾ pints) beef stock

Salt and freshly ground pepper

1. Warm the oil in a large saucepan over a medium heat. Add the onion, celery and carrot, season with a little salt and plenty of pepper and soften the vegetables for around 10 minutes.
2. Add the beef, tomatoes, barley and stock. Simmer for around 30 minutes until the ingredients are melded together nicely and the beef and barley are tender.
3. Taste and add more seasoning if it needs it. Ladle into bowls and serve hot.

★ This soup will keep for around 5 days in the fridge and will reheat well. Do not freeze this soup.

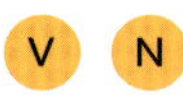

Pasta, Spinach & Yogurt Soup

This is an unusual soup but one that is full of flavour, really quick to make and very moreish. Spinach is a fantastic source of iron, calcium and vitamins. Make sure you use full-fat yogurt, so that it doesn't split when warmed.

SERVES 4–6

4 garlic cloves, chopped

2 tablespoons olive oil

1 litre (1¾ pints) vegetable stock

100g (3½oz) pasta shapes such as ditalini

8 tablespoons Greek-style yogurt

2 large handfuls of spinach leaves

Salt and freshly ground pepper, to taste

1. Put the garlic and oil into a large saucepan over a medium heat and warm until it smells fragrant. Add the stock and bring to the boil. Add the pasta and turn the heat down to a simmer. Cook for around 10 minutes, or until the pasta is tender.
2. Remove from the heat then add the yogurt and spinach leaves and stir until the spinach wilts. Taste and add some seasoning if it needs it. Serve immediately.

★ This soup is best eaten freshly made; it is not one to store, reheat or freeze.

Lentil, Tomato & Ras-El-Hanout Soup

I absolutely love to make this soup for a truly satisfying and flavoursome lunch or light supper. I first tried this combination of flavours when a friend served something very similar for supper at their house in Scotland on a freezing cold night. I loved it and have made it ever since. It works brilliantly with a range of extra toppings to add layers of additional flavours. I am particularly fond of adding some crumbled feta and fresh coriander leaves.

SERVES 4–6

4 tablespoons olive oil

1 onion, finely chopped

4 garlic cloves, finely chopped

1 heaped tablespoon ground cumin

1 tablespoon ground coriander

1 heaped tablespoon ras-el-hanout

275g (9¾oz) dried red lentils, rinsed

400g (14oz) can chopped tomatoes

1.2 litres (2 pints) vegetable stock

TO SERVE (OPTIONAL)

Crumbled feta

Flat-leaf parsley or coriander leaves

Squeeze of lemon juice

1. Warm the oil in a large saucepan over a medium heat and gently fry the onion until softened but not coloured. Add the garlic and spices and cook, stirring, for a minute, then add the lentils, tomatoes and stock. Bring to the boil, then reduce to a simmer and cook for around 30 minutes, or until the lentils are tender.
2. Taste, adjust the seasoning if it needs it, and serve, topped with feta and herbs, and a squeeze of lemon juice.

★ This soup will keep very well for up to 5 days in the fridge. It will also freeze and reheat well, before the toppings are added. Stir through a little more stock or water if it seems too thick.

Carrot, Lentil & Tahini

My sister made me soup along these lines for lunch one day and I enjoyed it so much, it stuck in my mind for a long time. Here I've attempted to recreate it, adding plenty of fresh ginger for zing, extra warmth and general good health.

SERVES 4–6

- 2 tablespoons olive or rapeseed oil
- 1 large onion, chopped
- 1 teaspoon whole cumin seeds
- 1 teaspoon whole coriander seeds
- 3 garlic cloves, chopped
- 3cm (1¼in) piece of fresh root ginger, peeled and chopped
- 550g (1lb 4oz) carrots, chopped
- 125g (4½oz) dried red lentils, rinsed
- 1.3 litres (2¼ pints) vegetable stock
- 125g (4½oz) tahini
- 1 tablespoon lemon juice
- Salt and freshly ground pepper

1. Warm the oil in a large saucepan over a low heat and gently fry the onion until softened but not coloured. Add the cumin, coriander, garlic and ginger and cook for another couple of minutes, before adding the carrots followed by the lentils. Season generously with salt and pepper.
2. Add the stock, bring to the boil and simmer for around 10–20 minutes until the lentils are soft.
3. Add the tahini and lemon juice and stir to combine. Blend the soup until smooth and silky. Taste, adjust the seasoning if it needs it, and serve straight away.

★ This soup will keep for up to 5 days in the fridge and will also freeze and reheat successfully. You may need to stir through a little more stock or water on reheating.

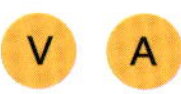

Sweet Potato, Lemongrass & Coconut Soup

Here you have a distinctive combination of flavours and one that, I think, works wonderfully together. Lemongrass is well worth acquiring to make this (and the stalks keep for quite a while in the fridge), adding a distinctive, almost fruity, note to the soup. This is one to make on a day when you fancy some lively flavours.

SERVES 4–6

- 1 tablespoon olive oil, butter or coconut oil
- 2 onions, thinly sliced
- 2 lemongrass stalks, outer layer peeled and thinly sliced
- 700g (1lb 9oz) sweet potatoes, cut into 1cm (½in) cubes
- 500ml (18fl oz) vegetable stock
- 400g (14oz) can full-fat coconut milk
- Salt

1. Put the oil, or butter, and onions into a large saucepan over a medium heat. Season with salt and gently fry for 20 minutes until softened but not coloured.
2. Add the lemongrass and sweet potatoes. Cover with stock and simmer for 15–20 minutes, until the potatoes are tender.
3. Stir in the coconut milk, warm through gently, then blend and taste to check the seasoning before serving – you may need a little more salt.

★ This soup will keep very happily for up to 5 days in the fridge. It reheats and freezes well too.

Beetroot, Ginger & Lime Soup

The combination of ginger and lime with fresh beetroot is really interesting. Beetroot is a good source of fibre as well as antioxidants and potassium. When blended, this soup has a velvety, rich texture and a striking pink colour.

SERVES 4–6

- 2 tablespoons olive oil
- 2 onions, sliced
- 2 garlic cloves, chopped
- 5cm (2in) piece of fresh root ginger, peeled and chopped
- 600g (1lb 5oz) fresh beetroot, peeled and chopped into 1cm (½in) cubes
- Zest of 1 unwaxed lime and the juice of ½
- 1 litre (1¾ pints) hot vegetable stock
- 1 tablespoon double or soured cream, plus extra to serve, if desired
- Salt and freshly ground pepper

1. Put the oil and onion into a large saucepan over a medium heat, season with salt and pepper and gently fry for around 10 minutes until the onion begins to soften.
2. Add the garlic, ginger and beetroot and cook for another 5 minutes until fragrant. Add the lime zest and juice and the stock, then simmer with a lid on for around 30 minutes until the beetroot cubes are tender.
3. Blend until smooth and stir in some cream, if you fancy it. Taste to check the seasoning, adding more salt and pepper if it needs it, then serve immediately. Some people may like an extra swirl of cream in their bowl.

★ This soup will keep for up to 5 days in the fridge and reheats well. It can be frozen, too.

5 Winter Warmers

N

Brazilian-Inspired Rice, Bean & Bacon Soup

If any recipe in this chapter is indeed a winter warmer, I feel this one is it. It's truly a real meal in a bowl. Perfect when you need some meaty warming comfort on a cold day or to feed those with a hearty appetite.

SERVES 4

1 tablespoon sunflower or rapeseed oil

1 large onion, finely chopped

2 garlic cloves, chopped

1 red chilli, deseeded and finely chopped (optional)

100g (3½oz) smoked back bacon, chopped

400g (14oz) can black beans, drained and rinsed

2 teaspoons fresh thyme

2 bay leaves

150g (5½oz) long-grain rice, rinsed

200ml (7fl oz) chicken stock

100g (3½oz) spring greens, thinly sliced

Squeeze of lime juice (optional)

Salt

15g (½oz) fresh coriander, chopped, to serve

1. Warm the oil in a large saucepan over a medium heat. Add the onion, season with a little salt and gently fry for around 10 minutes until softened but not coloured.
2. Add the garlic, chilli, bacon and beans. Fry, stirring, for another couple of minutes. Next add the thyme, bay leaves, rice and stock. Simmer for around 15–20 minutes until the rice is cooked.
3. Stir in the greens and cook for a further 5 minutes until they wilt slightly. Taste and add a little more salt and/or lime juice if it needs it. Ladle into bowls and serve hot, topped with fresh coriander.

★ This soup is best eaten on the day it is made.

N

Ginger Chicken Meatball Broth

This meatball broth is both light and satisfying – plus it's full of lively, Thai-inspired flavours.

SERVES 4–6

40g (1½oz) fresh coriander

4 garlic cloves, finely chopped

10cm (4in) piece of fresh root ginger, peeled and finely grated

500g (1lb 2oz) minced chicken or turkey

2½ tablespoons fish sauce

1 tablespoon oil

500ml (18fl oz) chicken or vegetable stock

Juice of 2 limes

1. First, make the meatballs. Take 25g (1oz) of the coriander and chop finely, then set the remaining leaves aside for a garnish. Mix together with the garlic, ginger, minced meat, and the fish sauce until evenly mixed. This can be done in a bowl by hand or in a food processor, if you have one. To form the meatballs, start by lightly wetting your hands with cold water. Pinch off walnut-sized balls of the mixture and roll them into neat balls. Put them on a plate, cover and refrigerate for up to an hour to firm up.
2. To assemble the broth, warm the stock in a large saucepan.
3. When you are ready to cook, warm the oil in a large frying pan over a medium–high heat. Fry the meatballs in the oil, turning regularly, until they are lightly brown on all sides. Work in batches if need be, to avoid overcrowding the pan.
4. Once all the meatballs are browned, put them into the hot stock and simmer for 5–10 minutes until they are fully cooked through. Finish by adding some fresh lime juice and the remaining coriander leaves to garnish. Ladle into bowls.

★ This soup is best served freshly made. It will reheat successfully, but only add the remaining coriander just before serving. Do not freeze this soup.

Ghanaian-Inspired Sweet Potato, Ginger & Peanut Soup

This fantastic soup with its rich, silky-smooth texture is a delight to eat. In Ghana, as in other West African countries, peanuts are often used in soups, typically with yams or plantain. Here, I'm using sweet potato. I recommend you use a richly flavoured peanut butter, such as a dark roast. The combination of flavours is interesting, layered and hugely enjoyable.

SERVES 6

2 tablespoons olive oil

1 onion, thinly sliced

2 garlic cloves, chopped

½ red chilli, deseeded and chopped

2 tablespoons peeled and grated fresh root ginger

1 tablespoon whole cumin seeds

1 large sweet potato (around 650g/1lb 7oz), peeled and diced

400g (14oz) can chopped tomatoes

1 litre (1¾ pints) vegetable stock

100g (3½oz) peanut butter

Salt

50g (1¾oz) salted peanuts, to serve (optional)

1. Warm the oil in a large, lidded saucepan over a medium heat. Add the onion, season with salt and fry, over a medium–high heat, for around 10 minutes, until it softens.
2. Add the garlic, chilli, ginger and cumin and fry for another couple of minutes until fragrant.
3. Add the sweet potato, tomatoes and stock. Simmer for around 20 minutes until the potato chunks are tender.
4. Finally, add the peanut butter and blend until smooth. Taste, adjust the seasoning, adding more salt if it needs it, and serve straight away, topped with peanuts, if you like.

★ This soup will keep well for up to 5 days in the fridge and will freeze very nicely, too.

Ramen

Ramen – noodle soup – is hugely popular in countries across the world. I read that it's actually a relatively new dish, introduced to Japan by Chinese settlers in the early twentieth century. This rich, savoury broth is designed to be a quick meal – and it can certainly be a complete one, given the various optional ingredients. Consider this recipe as an excellent base to which you can add as many or as few extras as you like. I personally prefer a simpler, more restrained approach, but feel free to add some or all of your favourite ingredients.

SERVES 4–6

75g (2¾oz) red or brown miso

1 litre (1¾ pints) chicken or vegetable stock or dashi

2–3 tablespoons toasted sesame oil, to taste

100g (3½oz) cooked ramen wheat noodles

300g (10½oz) silken tofu, drained and cut into cubes (optional)

TO SERVE

1 spring onion, sliced

2 tablespoons sesame seeds, toasted

Nori (dried seaweed sheets), sliced

Beansprouts

Lightly boiled eggs (or hard-boiled if you prefer), peeled and halved

Leftover roasted pork or chicken, sliced

Sweetcorn kernels

Pak choi, steamed

1. Warm the miso and stock in a saucepan over a medium heat. Whisk to ensure the miso dissolves into the liquid.
2. Add the sesame oil to taste, then add the cooked noodles and allow them to heat in the liquid for a minute.
3. Serve in bowls, with chunks of tofu and topped with your choice of additional ingredients.

★ This soup really is best eaten freshly made. The broth itself, though, will keep in the fridge for a couple of days then can be reheated and combined with freshly prepared additional ingredients. Do not freeze this soup.

Mexican-Inspired Bean, Tomato & Lime Soup with Avocado & Totopos

This is another light but really tasty broth with pleasing contrasting flavours and textures. Made with a vegetable stock, it is a great vegan meal in one, although in Mexico it might be made traditionally with a meat stock, so meat-eaters may prefer this option. And, in case you're wondering, totopos are triangles of corn tortilla that have been toasted, fried or baked. Specialist retailers sell them, but you can either make your own or use salted tortilla chips.

SERVES 4–6

2 tablespoons oil

1 large onion, finely chopped

4 garlic cloves, chopped

1 red chilli, deseeded and chopped

400g (14oz) can black beans, drained and rinsed

1 litre (1¾ pints) vegetable stock

Zest and juice of 1 unwaxed lime

200g (7oz) fresh tomatoes, chopped into 1cm (½in) dice

3 tablespoons chopped coriander, plus extra to serve

Salt

TO SERVE

1 ripe avocado, stoned, peeled and cut into 1cm (½in) dice

Fried totopos or salted tortilla chips (optional)

1. Warm the oil in a large saucepan over a medium heat. Add the onion, season with a little salt and gently fry for around 10 minutes, adjusting the heat so that the onion doesn't catch on the base or colour too much.
2. Add the garlic and chilli. Fry, stirring, for another couple of minutes, then add the beans and stock and simmer for around 15–20 minutes until the ingredients have melded together nicely and the beans and onions are tender.
3. Stir in half the lime zest and juice, the tomatoes and coriander. Taste and add a little more salt and/or lime if it needs it.
4. Ladle into bowls and serve hot, topped with coriander leaves, diced avocado and some crushed tortillas, if you wish.

★ This soup is best eaten freshly made. The soup base can be stored for up to 5 days in the fridge, or frozen and reheated but only add the coriander, avocado and tortilla just before serving.

N

Chorizo, Butter Bean & Cabbage Soup

This is a truly delicious winter soup that is really quick and easy to make. The trick, I think, with the cabbage, is to add it to the pan at the very last minute and stir through. This means that it will just soften, but retain its bite and colour. Here I've used chorizo but the soup would be excellent made with bacon, too.

SERVES 4

- 1 tablespoon good-quality olive oil
- 2 large onions, chopped
- 1 hoop of cured chorizo (around 200g/7oz), skinned and cut into 1cm (½in) cubes
- 400g (14oz) can butter beans, drained and rinsed
- 400g (14oz) can good-quality chopped tomatoes
- 1 litre (1¾ pints) chicken or vegetable stock
- Pinch of sugar (optional)
- ½ Savoy cabbage, thinly sliced and tough stalks discarded
- Salt and freshly ground pepper
- Chopped parsley, to serve (optional)

1. Add the oil and onions to a large saucepan over a medium heat. Gently fry for 5–10 minutes at least, until the onions soften slightly.
2. Add the chorizo, season with salt and pepper, and continue to fry for another 5–10 minutes, until the fat starts to render from the chorizo.
3. Next, stir through the butter beans and tomatoes, followed by the stock. Simmer with a lid on for 15 minutes or so, to allow the flavours to combine.
4. Taste to check the soup is sweet and flavourful – it may need another 10 minutes if the tomatoes still taste acidic and raw. You can add a little sugar to help it along.
5. Add the sliced cabbage. Stir well and gently simmer for another 3 minutes or so, until it has just softened – no need to put the lid back on once the cabbage is in the pan. Taste and check that the cabbage is cooked to your liking and the soup is adequately seasoned. Serve immediately, sprinkled with parsley, if you wish.

Spiced Cauliflower & Chickpea Soup

Inspired by the flavours of southern Spain where cumin, cauliflower and olive oil are often used together, this is a tasty and warming soup with a creamy mouthfeel from the chickpeas.

SERVES 4–6

2 tablespoons olive oil, plus extra to serve

1 large onion, chopped

1 heaped tablespoon whole cumin seeds

1 large head of cauliflower, stalk included, trimmed and chopped

400g (14oz) can chickpeas, drained

1.2 litres (2 pints) vegetable stock

Squeeze of lemon juice

Salt and freshly ground pepper

1. Warm the oil in a large, lidded saucepan over a medium heat. Add the onion and cumin seeds, season with salt and pepper and fry, stirring, for around 10 minutes until the cumin smells fragrant and the onion has softened a little.
2. Add the cauliflower, chickpeas and stock and bring to the boil, put the lid on and simmer for around 20 minutes or until the cauliflower is tender.
3. Blend the soup until smooth, add the lemon juice, taste and season with extra salt and pepper if needed. Serve immediately, drizzled with a little extra olive oil, if you like.

★ This soup will keep for up to 5 days in the fridge and it freezes well.

Turkey, Barley & Vegetable Soup

This is a really simple traditional soup, which is full of flavour, hugely nourishing and comforting. Use uncooked or roasted turkey breast or leg, whichever you have. Should you find yourself with leftover turkey meat and bones during the festive season, you might like to make your own stock by substituting turkey bones for chicken in my chicken stock recipe (see page 161).

SERVES 4–6

1 tablespoon olive oil
1 onion, chopped
1 large carrot, chopped
2 celery sticks, trimmed and sliced
300g (10½oz) pearl barley
300g (10½oz) uncooked or roasted turkey meat, chopped or sliced
1.5 litres (scant 2¾ pints) turkey, chicken or vegetable stock
Salt and freshly ground pepper

1. Warm the oil in a large saucepan over a medium heat. Add the onion and fry for around 10 minutes until it starts to soften.
2. Add the carrot and celery and fry for a further 5 minutes. Season with salt and pepper.
3. Add the pearl barley, turkey meat and stock and simmer for 30–45 minutes until the barley is tender. Taste, adjust the seasoning, adding salt and pepper if it needs it, then serve immediately.

★ This soup will keep for up to 5 days in the fridge and will reheat well.

Bessara

This soup is full of savoury flavours and it's inspired by the wonderful Moroccan dish bessara, which is made with dried fava beans or, as I use here, yellow split peas. One of the many reasons I love this soup is because it contains plenty of fresh greens which have a wonderful flavour and texture. I am always amazed that such simple ingredients can taste so good.

SERVES 4–6

2 tablespoons olive oil

2 onions, chopped

2 carrots, chopped

2 celery sticks, trimmed and chopped

1 heaped teaspoon whole cumin seeds

300g (10½oz) dried yellow split peas

1.25 litres (generous 2 pints) vegetable stock

Juice of ½ lemon

100g (3½oz) spring greens, thinly sliced

Salt and freshly ground pepper

10g (¼oz) coriander leaves, to serve

1. Warm the oil in a large saucepan over a medium heat. Add the onions and fry for around 3 minutes until they start to look translucent.
2. Add the carrots and celery and season with salt and pepper. Add the cumin seeds and split peas. Stir everything together. Pour in the stock, bring to the boil then simmer for at least 30 minutes, until the lentils are tender.
3. Add the lemon juice and blend, if desired. Taste and adjust the seasoning with more salt and pepper if it needs it.
4. Stir in the spring greens and leave for a few minutes for them to wilt. Serve immediately, topped with fresh coriander.

★ This soup will keep for up to 5 days in the fridge. It will freeze and reheat very successfully, but only add the greens and coriander when reheating to retain the best flavour and texture.

Spiced Butternut Squash & Lentil Soup

This soup is ideal for the winter months, packed with health-giving spices, vegetables and lentils, making it a sustaining and well-balanced meal in a bowl. I make this with butternut squash but other types, such as Crown Prince or Kuri, work just as well.

SERVES 4–6

2 tablespoons olive or rapeseed oil

1 large onion, chopped

1 tablespoon ground cumin

1 tablespoon ground coriander

1 teaspoon ground turmeric

4 garlic cloves, chopped

3cm (1¼in) piece of fresh root ginger, peeled and chopped

400g (14oz) butternut or other type of squash, peeled, deseeded and chopped

150g (5½oz) dried red lentils, rinsed

800ml (scant 1½ pints) vegetable stock

1 tablespoon lemon juice

Salt and freshly ground pepper

1. Add the oil and chopped onion to a large saucepan over a gentle heat and fry until the onion is softened but not coloured.
2. Stir through the cumin, coriander, turmeric, garlic and ginger, and cook for 2 minutes, before adding the squash followed by the lentils. Season generously with salt and pepper. Add the stock, bring to the boil and simmer for around 20 minutes until the squash and lentils are tender.
3. Add the lemon juice and stir to combine. Blend the soup until smooth. Taste, adjust the seasoning if it needs it, and serve straight away.

★ This soup will keep for up to 5 days in the fridge and will freeze and reheat successfully.

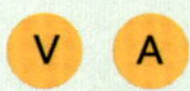

Leek & Celeriac Soup

This is a lovely creamy, gentle and warming soup. Celeriac has a wonderful celery-like flavour and is in season from autumn all the way through to spring. The leeks and celeriac offer a fantastic combination of sweet, earthy and nutty flavours which are so enjoyable.

SERVES 4–6

75g (2¾oz) butter or 3 tablespoons olive oil

2 leeks, trimmed and thinly sliced

2 garlic cloves, chopped

1 celeriac, peeled and diced (you want around 400g (14oz) prepared weight)

1 litre (1¾ pints) vegetable stock

200ml (7fl oz) milk

Salt and freshly ground pepper

1. Melt the butter, or warm the oil, in a large saucepan over a medium heat. Add the leeks and garlic and fry for around 10 minutes until they start to soften. Season with salt and pepper and stir well.
2. Add the celeriac and stock, bring to the boil then simmer for around 20 minutes until the vegetables are tender. Add the milk and blend until smooth.
3. Taste and check the seasoning. It may need a little more salt and pepper. Serve hot.

★ This soup will keep for up to 5 days in the fridge and will freeze and reheat extremely well.

Parsnip, Rosemary & Olive Soup

This one is a personal favourite of mine. I love the combination of sweet parsnips, the green, almost resinous, taste of fresh rosemary, and salty black olives. It's an unusual but moreish set of flavours and I find myself drawn to making this soup again and again.

SERVES 4–6

2 tablespoons olive oil

1 leek, trimmed and thinly sliced

400g (14oz) parsnips, peeled and cut into 1cm (½in) chunks

4 garlic cloves, chopped

2 tablespoons chopped rosemary needles

850ml (1½ pints) vegetable stock

75g (2¾oz) pitted black olives, chopped

Salt and freshly ground pepper

1. Put the oil and leek into a large, lidded saucepan over a medium heat, season with salt and pepper and fry for around 10 minutes until the leek starts to soften.
2. Add the parsnips, garlic and rosemary and season with a little pepper. Cook for another 5 minutes until fragrant.
3. Add the stock, then simmer with a lid on for around 30 minutes until the parsnips are tender.
4. Blend until smooth and stir in the olives. Taste to check the seasoning and serve immediately.

★ This soup will keep for up to 5 days stored in the fridge and reheats well. It can be frozen successfully, but I recommend you only add the olives when reheating the soup just before serving.

6
Oven-Baked

Roasted Cauliflower, Almond & Turmeric Soup

This is a rich and creamy soup with a gentle but interesting flavour. Ground almonds help to thicken the soup and turmeric adds its warmth and vivid colour.

SERVES 4–6

1 large cauliflower, cut into florets

1 large onion, quartered

1 teaspoon ground turmeric

½ teaspoon ground ginger

1 tablespoon sunflower or rapeseed oil

1 teaspoon salt

70g (2½oz) ground almonds

1 litre (1¾ pints) vegetable stock

300ml (10fl oz) milk

Freshly ground pepper

1. Preheat the oven to 180°C/160°C fan (350°F), Gas Mark 4.
2. Put the cauliflower and onion into a large ovenproof dish, sprinkle with turmeric and ground ginger, drizzle with oil and season with salt and pepper. Roast for around 35 minutes until tender and lightly browned, turning the vegetables after about 18 minutes to ensure they cook evenly. Towards the very end of the cooking time, add the almonds to the dish and roast for a further 5–8 minutes until toasted.
3. Transfer the roasted vegetables to a large saucepan and pour in the stock. Bring to a simmer over a medium heat and cook for around 10 minutes.
4. Add the milk, bring back to a simmer, then blend until smooth. Taste, adjust the seasoning if it needs it, and serve immediately.

★ This soup will keep for up to 5 days in the fridge and reheats nicely, but do not freeze it.

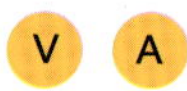

Roasted Butternut Squash & Blue Cheese Soup

Many of you may have enjoyed blue cheese in a broccoli and Stilton soup. It pairs wonderfully well with squash, too – this is a real favourite of mine. Everyone who has tasted it says how much they like the combination of flavours.

SERVES 4–6

1 onion, cut into wedges

500g (1lb 2oz) butternut or other type of squash, peeled and cut into 2cm (¾in) chunks

1 tablespoon olive oil

600ml (20fl oz) hot vegetable stock

100g (3½oz) blue cheese, such as Stilton, crumbled, plus extra to serve

Salt and freshly ground pepper

1. Preheat the oven to 180°C/160°C fan (350°F), Gas Mark 4.
2. Put the onion and squash into a large ovenproof dish, drizzle with olive oil and season with salt and pepper. Roast for around 40 minutes until tender and lightly browned. Turn the vegetables after about 20 minutes to ensure they cook evenly.
3. Transfer the roasted vegetables to a large saucepan, pour in the stock and add the cheese. Bring to a simmer over a medium heat and cook for around 10 minutes.
4. Blend until smooth. Check the seasoning, then serve scattered with extra Stilton.

★ This soup will keep for up to 5 days in the fridge and reheats nicely. It will also freeze very well.

Roasted Pumpkin & Rosemary Soup

Seasonal pumpkin makes a fantastic soup and roasting it really helps to bring out the best flavour. Pairing pumpkin with rosemary is a very happy marriage. I also like to serve this soup topped with some crispy fresh sage leaves, which have been briefly fried in a little hot oil.

SERVES 4–6

1 large onion, thickly sliced

600g (1lb 5oz) pumpkin or squash, peeled, deseeded and chopped

1 tablespoon chopped rosemary needles

3 garlic cloves, unpeeled

2 tablespoons olive oil

1 litre (1¾ pints) hot vegetable stock

Salt and freshly ground pepper

1. Preheat the oven to 180°C/160°C fan (350°F), Gas Mark 4.
2. Put the onion, pumpkin, rosemary and garlic on a roasting tray, drizzle with oil, season with salt and pepper and cover with foil. Roast for 45 minutes until everything is tender and remove from the oven. When cool enough to handle, squeeze the garlic cloves out of the skins and discard the skin.
3. When you're ready to finish the soup, bring the stock to the boil in a large saucepan – one big enough to accommodate the roasted vegetables. Add the vegetables from the tray and simmer for 10 minutes.
4. Remove from the heat and blend until smooth. Taste and adjust the seasoning if needed and serve hot.

★ This soup will keep for up to 5 days in the fridge. It will reheat very well and will also freeze.

Roasted Tomato, Coconut & Basil Soup

Tomato and basil are a classic combination in various cuisines, not least Italian, but they pair amazingly well with coconut, too. I am really fond of this trio of ingredients. This is another soup that I've found to be popular with children and adults alike.

SERVES 4–6

900g (2lb) tomatoes, cored and quartered

4 garlic cloves, peeled

1 large onion, thickly sliced

4 fresh basil sprigs, plus extra to serve

2–3 tablespoons extra virgin olive oil

2 teaspoons sugar

500ml (18fl oz) vegetable stock

400g (14oz) can full-fat coconut milk

Salt and freshly ground pepper

1. Preheat the oven to 230°C/210°C fan (450°F), Gas Mark 8. Line a large baking tray (or 2 if you need more space) with baking paper.
2. Put the tomatoes, garlic, onion and basil sprigs onto the tray(s). Drizzle over the oil and season with salt, pepper and sugar. Toss the ingredients to coat them evenly with the oil and seasoning and roast for around 20–30 minutes until the onion is soft and the tomatoes are sweet and tender.
3. Meanwhile, gently warm the stock and coconut milk together in a large saucepan – one big enough to accommodate the roasted vegetables.
4. Once the vegetables are roasted, transfer them immediately to the warm stock and coconut milk in the pan. Blend until smooth. Taste, adjust the seasoning if it needs it, and serve topped with more fresh basil.

★ This soup will keep for up to 5 days in the fridge, ready to be reheated when needed. Don't add the fresh basil garnish before you ladle the hot soup into bowls, though, otherwise it will deteriorate. Do not freeze this soup.

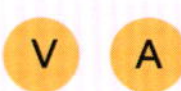

Cumin & Honey-Roasted Carrot Soup

The combination of cumin, carrots and honey is a wonderful marriage of flavours and using the oven makes it so easy to make this soup. You can batch-cook this then freeze it to enjoy on another day.

SERVES 4–6

- 1 large onion, thickly sliced
- 750g (1lb 10oz) carrots, chopped
- 1 tablespoon cumin seeds
- 1 tablespoon olive oil
- 1 tablespoon runny honey
- 1 litre (1¾ pints) hot vegetable stock
- Salt and freshly ground pepper

1. Preheat the oven to 180°C/160°C fan (350°F), Gas Mark 4.
2. Put the onion, carrots and cumin seeds on a roasting tray, drizzle with oil, season with salt and pepper and cover with foil. Roast for 40 minutes until tender. Remove the foil, drizzle over the honey and roast for a further 5 minutes.
3. When you're ready to finish the soup, transfer all the roasted vegetables and cumin seeds to a large saucepan. Pour in the stock and simmer for 10 minutes.
4. Blend until smooth. Taste and adjust the seasoning if needed and serve hot.

★ This soup will keep for up to 5 days in the fridge, ready to reheat, and also freezes very happily.

Roasted Root Vegetable Soup

I don't know how such a simple soup can taste so good! This one is full of sweet, roasted vegetables. I think it's one of the healthiest and most comforting recipes in the book.

SERVES 4–6

- 1 onion, cut into wedges
- 200g (7oz) parsnips, cut into 2cm (¾in) chunks
- 200g (7oz) carrots, cut into 2cm (¾in) chunks
- 200g (7oz) swede, cut into 2cm (¾in) cubes
- 1 tablespoon olive oil
- 850ml (1½ pints) hot vegetable stock
- Salt and freshly ground pepper

1. Preheat the oven to 180°C/160°C fan (350°F), Gas Mark 4.
2. Put the onion, parsnip, carrot and swede into a large ovenproof dish, drizzle with olive oil and season with salt and pepper. Roast for around 40 minutes until tender and lightly browned. Turn the vegetables after about 20 minutes to ensure they cook evenly.
3. Transfer the roasted vegetables to a large saucepan and pour in the stock. Bring to a simmer and cook for around 10 minutes until everything is heated through.
4. Remove from the heat and blend until smooth. Check the seasoning and serve immediately.

★ This soup will keep for up to 5 days in the fridge. It reheats nicely and also freezes very well.

Roasted Beetroot & Apple Soup

The combination of roasted beetroot and apple is fantastic in a soup: the earthiness and sweetness from these ingredients is a delight. Be sure to cut the beetroot into cubes smaller than the apple, so that the root vegetable will be fully roasted within the time.

SERVES 4–6

1 large onion, thickly sliced

600g (1lb 5oz) beetroot, peeled and chopped into 1–2cm (½–¾in) cubes

2 celery sticks, trimmed and sliced

2 eating apples, cored and cut into 3cm (1¼in) chunks

4 tablespoons olive oil

1 litre (1¾ pints) hot vegetable stock

Salt and freshly ground pepper

Cream or soured cream, to serve (optional)

1. Preheat the oven to 180°C/160°C fan (350°F), Gas Mark 4.
2. Put the onion, beetroot, celery and apple on a roasting tray, drizzle with oil, season with salt and pepper and cover with foil. Roast for 45 minutes or until tender.
3. When you're ready to finish the soup, transfer all the roasted vegetables into a large saucepan, pour in the hot stock and simmer over a medium heat for 10 minutes.
4. Remove from the heat and blend until smooth. Taste and adjust the seasoning if needed and serve hot. I like a dash of cream or soured cream stirred into the soup at the table.

★ This soup will keep for up to 5 days in the fridge. It will freeze and reheat extremely well.

Thai-Inspired Squash & Coconut Soup

The flavours of green Thai curry paste pair so nicely with roasted squash and coconut. This is an easy soup to make and scales up very well – ideal if you're feeding a crowd. Do check that your green Thai curry paste is suitable for vegetarians.

SERVES 4–6

500g (1lb 2oz) butternut or other type of squash, peeled, deseeded and diced

1 onion, cut into wedges

1 tablespoon sunflower or rapeseed oil

Salt

1 tablespoon green Thai curry paste (vegetarian)

1 tablespoon brown sugar

400ml (14fl oz) vegetable stock

2 makrut lime leaves

400g (14oz) can full-fat coconut milk

Squeeze of lime juice (optional)

1. Preheat the oven to 180°C/160°C fan (350°F), Gas Mark 4.
2. Put the squash and onion into a large ovenproof dish, drizzle with olive oil and season with salt. Roast for around 40 minutes until tender and lightly browned. Turn the vegetables after about 20 minutes to ensure they cook evenly.
3. Add the green Thai curry paste to a large saucepan and warm it through over a medium heat, stirring constantly for around a minute.
4. Add the sugar, stock, lime leaves and coconut milk, stir well then add the roasted squash and onion. Bring to a simmer and cook for around 10 minutes until everything is heated through.
5. Remove from the heat, discard the lime leaves and blend until smooth. Check the seasoning and add a dash of lime juice, if you would like a little acidity. Serve immediately.

★ This soup will keep for up to 5 days in the fridge. It reheats nicely and also freezes very well.

7

Finishing Touches

Fresh Pesto – Three Ways

A spoonful of herb pesto makes a delicious topping to add to a bowl of soup with its fresh and vibrant flavour. All three pestos here can be stored in the fridge for up to 5 days. Add a tablespoon or two of oil over the surface to form a protective layer that will prevent any discolouration, to which basil pesto particularly is prone.

Basil Pesto

ENOUGH FOR 8–10, AS A TOPPING

1 garlic clove, halved

75g (2¾oz) fresh basil, leaves and soft stems

50g (1¾oz) Parmesan-style vegetarian cheese, grated

50g (1¾oz) pine nuts, toasted

about 150ml (5fl oz) extra virgin olive oil

Salt and freshly ground pepper

1. Put all the ingredients in a blender (or a jug if you are using a stick blender) and whizz until the basil is broken down but the nuts still have some texture (alternatively, pound the ingredients together using a pestle and mortar). A nubbly texture looks very pleasing, but continue to blend until smooth, if you prefer.
2. Taste and add more salt, if needed. Stir through a little more oil if you wish to loosen the consistency, too. Ideally, serve straight away, or store in a sealed jar in the fridge.

Parsley Pesto

ENOUGH FOR 8–10, AS A TOPPING

1 garlic clove, halved

75g (2¾oz) fresh parsley, leaves and stems

50g (1¾oz) Parmesan-style vegetarian cheese, grated

about 150ml (5fl oz) extra virgin olive oil

Large pinch of salt

1. Put all the ingredients in a blender (or a jug if you are using a stick blender) and whizz together until evenly combined (alternatively, pound the ingredients together using a pestle and mortar).
2. Taste and adjust the salt if it needs a little more, or add extra oil to loosen the consistency. Ideally, serve straight away, or store in a sealed jar in the fridge.

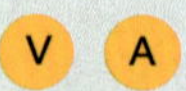

Pumpkin Seed Pesto

ENOUGH FOR 8–10, AS A TOPPING

1 garlic clove, halved

75g (2¾oz) fresh parsley, leaves and stems

50g (1¾oz) Parmesan-style vegetarian cheese, grated

50g (1¾oz) pumpkin seeds, toasted

150ml (5fl oz) extra virgin olive oil

Salt and freshly ground pepper

1. Put all the ingredients in a blender (or a jug if you are using a stick blender) and whizz together until the pesto is fairly smooth (alternatively, pound the ingredients together using a pestle and mortar).
2. Taste and adjust the salt, if needed. Add a little more oil, if you feel the consistency needs loosening. Ideally, serve straight away, or store in a sealed jar in the fridge.

Crispy Bacon Sprinkle

This is a wonderful topping to add to soups of all kinds. Think of it more as a technique, rather than a recipe, so you can make as much, or as little, as you need. While it will keep for a couple of days in the fridge, it is most crispy when freshly made, so this isn't really a recipe to cook ahead of time. Use smoked or unsmoked bacon, whichever you prefer, but streaky will give you a crisper result than back bacon.

SERVES 4

8 streaky bacon rashers

1. Preheat the grill to medium–high. Line a grill tray with foil and lay the bacon rashers on the grill rack.
2. Once the grill is hot, grill the bacon until crisp and richly coloured, turning it as soon as the top turns golden brown. Remove from the grill and set aside to cool a little so that it crisps up further.
3. Break the rashers into pieces and serve straight away.

Garlic Yogurt

Tart and refreshing, a simple swirl of this pungent yogurt is a welcome topping to serve at the table. Be sure to use full-fat yogurt.

ENOUGH TO TOP 4 BOWLS OF SOUP

4 tablespoons Greek yogurt
2 tablespoons olive oil
1 garlic clove, crushed
Salt

1. Mix the ingredients together in a bowl. Taste and add a little more salt, if needed. Covered, this will keep for up to 5 days in the fridge.

Toasted Seed Mix

Toasting seeds enhances their nutty flavour and delivers a crisp crunch, and a sprinkling of seeds over a bowl of soup adds a wonderful layer of contrasting textures. I recommend making these in batches to suit your needs as they lose their freshness after a week, even kept in a sealed container. This is another template recipe, so feel free to use any proportions of seeds you prefer.

MAKES AROUND 400G (14OZ), ENOUGH FOR 1 LARGE JAR

150g (5½oz) pumpkin seeds
100g (3½oz) sesame seeds, black, white or a mix of both
25g (1oz) poppy seeds
10g (¼oz) nigella seeds
100g (3½oz) pine nuts (optional)

1. For best results, toast each type of seed (and the pine nuts, if you're using them) separately in a dry frying pan over a medium–high heat until lightly brown and crisp. Watch them carefully as they can easily burn, and shake the pan from time to time.
2. Mix the toasted seeds together and eat straight away or, once they are cool, store in a sealed jar or an airtight container for up to a week.

Herb Oil

A drizzle of oil is sometimes all you need to dress a bowl of soup. The flavours of the fresh herbs really enhance the oil, and add a beautiful visual flourish, too.

ENOUGH FOR 4–6, AS A TOPPING

2 heaped tablespoons chopped fresh herbs, such as rosemary, parsley, coriander or basil

50ml (2fl oz) olive oil

1. Simply stir or blend the herbs and oil together and serve immediately or pour into a clean jar and seal tightly.

★ Rosemary oil will keep for a few days; parsley or coriander oil for 2 days. Basil oil, however, is best used immediately.

Crispy Chilli Oil

This is a wonderful, punchy way to finish a soup. Simply shake the oil and spoon a little over each serving. A bottle of this oil also makes a wonderful gift, so do scale up the quantities you cook for that purpose.

ENOUGH FOR 4–6, AS A TOPPING

200ml (7fl oz) sunflower oil or rapeseed oil

2 tablespoons Szechuan peppercorns

30g (1oz) chilli flakes

5 star anise

1 cinnamon stick

1 teaspoon cloves

2 black cardamom pods

1 teaspoon salt

1. Put all the ingredients into a small saucepan over a low heat. Stir and simmer for 30 minutes until the chilli flakes turn crispy. Allow to cool and store until needed.

★ This chilli oil will keep in a sealed jar or bottle in the fridge for up to 2 weeks.

Cheese Scones

These scones are such a crowd-pleaser and will be sure to appeal to people of all ages. This makes a large batch because they usually disappear rather quickly. Since these are best eaten on the day they are made, I often cut any leftovers in half and freeze them which preserves them better. They will defrost in a couple of hours at room temperature, but when I really can't wait, I'll stick them in the toaster then butter them – delicious!

MAKES ABOUT 12 LARGE SCONES

450g (1lb) self-raising flour, plus extra for dusting

1 heaped teaspoon mustard powder (optional)

Pinch of fine salt

100g (3½oz) cold butter, cubed

175g (6oz) mature Cheddar cheese, grated

300ml (10fl oz) milk, plus an extra tablespoon, for brushing

1. Preheat the oven to 220°C/200°C (425°F), Gas Mark 7. Line a large baking tray with nonstick baking paper and set aside.
2. Put the flour, salt and butter in a large mixing bowl. Rub the butter into the flour until it looks like rough breadcrumbs. Stir in 125g (4½oz) of the grated Cheddar, reserving the remaining 50g (2oz) to top the scones.
3. Add the milk and stir using a spatula to bring the mixture together, forming a soft dough.
4. Lightly flour a work surface and turn out the dough onto the floured area. Roll in the flour to coat the sticky dough and make it easier to handle. Press or roll the dough into a disc or square, around 4cm (1½in) thick. Use a large knife to cut into triangles or squares. Alternatively, stamp into rounds using a cutter around 6cm (2½in). Gather the leftover dough together and repeat to use all of the dough.
5. Brush the tops of the scones with milk (not the sides, as this can stop them rising properly) and top with the remaining cheese.
6. Bake the scones for around 12–17 minutes until well-risen and golden. Eat warm, or preferably on the day of baking. Leftovers will freeze very well.

Fluffy, Puffy Flatbreads

This is such a useful recipe for making thick, light, fluffy flatbreads. They are so good eaten with soup (especially for mopping up the bowl!), but they go with lots of other dishes – I often serve them with curries, stews and salads. This recipe makes a good batch so I often freeze some. They defrost quickly and work wonderfully well toasted from frozen, too.

MAKES 8–12

2 tablespoons sunflower or rapeseed oil

300ml (10fl oz) Greek yogurt

4 tablespoons cold water

600g (1lb 5oz) self-raising flour, plus extra for dusting

1 teaspoon baking powder

1 teaspoon fine salt

1. Put the oil, yogurt and water into a medium bowl and stir well.
2. Sift the flour, baking powder and salt into a large mixing bowl. Add in the wet ingredients and stir well to bring the mixture together. You might need a dash of extra water if it looks a little dry.
3. Roll the dough in a little flour to make it easier to handle and knead it very lightly for around a minute. Divide into pieces (as large or small as you want).
4. Preheat a dry nonstick frying pan over a medium–high heat.
5. Roll the dough pieces into discs around 5–8mm (a good ¼ inch) thick. Cook the flatbreads, in batches, in the preheated frying pan for around 2 minutes on each side, until golden and puffy. Transfer to a wire rack to cool briefly before serving.

★ The flatbreads are great eaten fresh out of the pan but they freeze brilliantly. I often defrost and warm them in the toaster.

Fougasse

This is a yeasted bread from the south of France. With its leaf-like shape it looks really impressive and yet it is much quicker to make than many yeasted breads. The instructions may seem involved but it's all about getting the technique right, and I hope you will master this first time. Once you know what you're doing, it becomes a doddle to make fougasse again and again. The recipe makes two loaves that will cook at the same time. They freeze beautifully and defrost within a few hours at room temperature.

MAKES 2 LOAVES

1kg (2lb 4oz) strong white bread flour, plus extra for kneading and shaping

1 teaspoon fast-action dried yeast

2 teaspoons salt

700ml (1¼ pints) tepid water

1. Mix the flour, yeast and salt together in a large mixing bowl. Make a well in the centre and pour in the water. Mix together using your hands or a spatula (less messy!), gradually incorporating the dry ingredients into the liquid until you have a sticky dough.
2. Flour the work surface and transfer the dough to the floured area. Keep the mixing bowl to hand for later. Roll the dough in flour so that the sticky surfaces become easier to handle. Knead the dough for 5–10 minutes until smooth. Try not to add extra flour if you can avoid it – the dough will become less sticky as it is kneaded. As an alternative, you can knead the dough in a stand mixer fitted with a dough hook, if you have one.
3. Place the dough back in the mixing bowl. Cover and leave it in a warm place to prove and double in size. This may take up to 1½ hours, depending on the ambient temperature.
4. Once the dough has risen, preheat the oven to 220°C/200°C fan (425°F), Gas Mark 7.
5. Gently turn out the proved dough onto a well-floured surface and flour the top of the dough. Using a plastic scraper or dough cutter, divide the dough into 2.

Continued overleaf

6. To shape the fougasse, use your hands to shape and slightly flatten each piece of dough into an oval. At this stage, I like to transfer them to a baking tray. Make 1 large cut down the centre, almost the full length of the dough but leave 2–3cm (¾–1¼in) at each end, so that it remains in one piece. Make sure you cut all the way through the dough so it separates. (A plastic dough scraper is a useful tool to use here, so that you don't damage your baking tray. Or, if you don't have a dough scraper, you can do this on a sheet of nonstick baking paper that you can slide easily onto the baking tray.) Flour the cut edges of the dough and pull them apart.

7. Next, make another 2–3 diagonal cuts on either side of the long central cut you just made, like the veins of a leaf. Make these cuts long, but without touching the central cut or cutting through the edge of the loaf. As before, flour the cut edges of the dough and pull them apart.

8. Once both loaves are shaped, put them into the oven straight away. They should take around 10–16 minutes to bake, depending on the thickness of the dough and your oven. The bread will puff quite considerably in the oven (which is why you need to pull apart the cuts), and when it is a pleasing mid-brown colour, it should be ready to remove from the oven and cool.

★ This is a great bread to serve in the middle of the table for everyone to admire and then tear apart to accompany their soup.

Focaccia

Focaccia is a popular yeasted Italian bread and it's another good bread to make from scratch at home. There are a number of different regional varieties of focaccia across the country. This is my preferred version, a Roman-style focaccia, which is characterized by particularly large air bubbles and an irresistible sprinkle of salt on top. I particularly like to make this bread when I'm cooking for friends and family because it's unfailingly popular and is such a treat to eat when served warm, freshly baked from the oven. It can be happily served on its own, or perhaps with an extra drizzle of olive oil. Although the flavour of the olive oil and salt comes through nicely, this is still quite a neutral-tasting bread, so it can be paired with a really wide range of soups. This focaccia is not too tricky to make, but bear in mind that the dough should be very wet. That can make it harder to handle, but the result is a wonderfully tender crumb. Use a spatula or stand mixer to mix the dough to avoid getting in a mess. Slightly wet hands help, too.

SERVES 8

525g (1lb 3oz) strong white bread flour

1 heaped teaspoon flaky salt, plus extra to finish

1 teaspoon fast-action dried yeast

400ml (14fl oz) tepid water

12 tablespoons olive oil – half for the dough and half for drizzling

1. Put the dry ingredients into a large mixing bowl and stir well to mix to ensure they are evenly dispersed – a whisk does this job very effectively. Add the water and 6 tablespoons of olive oil and stir to form a sticky dough.
2. To knead the dough, mix well using a spatula until the dough starts to look smooth and even. (Alternatively, you can knead the dough in a stand mixer fitted with a dough hook, if you have one. Usually, the dough will need to be kneaded for less time in a stand mixer than by hand.)
3. Leave the dough in the mixing bowl, covered with clingfilm, in a warm place for at least 1 hour to rise and double in size.

Continued overleaf

4. Drizzle a little olive oil over the bottom of your largest baking tray (with sides). Tip the focaccia dough into the tray and use your fingers to gently push and tease it into the edges of the tray – you want a rectangular shape about 5cm (2in) thick. Dipping your fingertips in a little oil first will prevent them from sticking to the dough as you work. Drizzle over a little more oil, cover with clingfilm and leave it to prove for another hour.
5. When the hour is nearly up, preheat the oven to 220°C/200°C fan (425°F), Gas Mark 7. Uncover the focaccia dough, drizzle with more oil and use your fingertips to press into the dough to form deep indents. Dipping your fingertips in a little oil first will prevent them from sticking to the dough as you work. Sprinkle generously with flaky sea salt.
6. Bake the bread for 25–35 minutes until it's mid-brown in colour, crisp on the bottom and feels light. You might wish to remove it from the sheet and bake for the final 5–10 minutes directly on the oven shelf, for extra crispness. Turn out onto a wire rack and enjoy as soon as it's cool enough to handle with more olive oil for dipping, if you like.

★ Focaccia is best eaten very fresh, so after day one, I cut any leftovers into 1cm (½in) thick slices and put them in the freezer. The slices can later be defrosted and warmed in a toaster: perfect to serve with soup when time is in short supply!

V

Cheesy Wheaten Farls

This is my take on the delicious griddle breads of Northern Ireland, which were traditionally made by most households to use up milk and could be made very quickly on a stove top. They can still still be found in most bakeries today and are often freshly made at food markets, so do look out for them if you happen to be visiting. Because they don't keep for long, they are a type of bread that is baked daily and should be eaten very fresh. These farls are so quick to make and there's no need to knead, prove or even turn the oven on – they cook in a dry frying pan on the hob. I made them on repeat when my kitchen was being renovated and I had no oven for a time. For best results, you need a good nonstick pan, so do try and find the right one for this recipe. This cheesy bread is best eaten while still warm, either buttered or just as it is. Pair with any soup recipe that you feel will suit the wonderfully cheesy flavour. Any leftovers are good sliced and toasted.

SERVES 4–8

250–325ml (9–11fl oz) buttermilk or milk

1 tablespoon lemon juice (only required if using milk)

350g (12oz) plain flour, plus extra for dusting

1 teaspoon salt

1 teaspoon bicarbonate of soda

150g (5½oz) mature Cheddar cheese, grated

1. If you don't have any buttermilk, it is very easy to make your own. Put the milk into a jug and add the lemon juice. Let it sit for about 5 minutes until it thickens a little, and then it will be ready to use. If it looks a little lumpy, that's absolutely fine.
2. Sift the dry ingredients into a mixing bowl and stir in the grated Cheddar. Make a well in the centre and pour in almost all of the buttermilk. Using a spatula, gently mix until the dry ingredients are incorporated into the buttermilk to form a sticky dough. Add the rest of the liquid only if needed (the amount of liquid you need may vary a little depending on how absorbent your flour is, so don't be afraid to use your judgement here).
3. Flour your work surface generously and turn out the sticky ball of dough onto the floured area. Roll it in flour to make it easier to handle and use your hands to gently shape and flatten it to form a fat disc, around 5cm (2in) thick.

4. Preheat a dry nonstick frying pan over a medium–high heat. No fat or oil is needed – you just want get the dry pan really warm (but not smoking hot!) before cooking.

5. You can cook the farl whole or cut it into quarters before cooking. Transfer the dough carefully into the preheated pan and immediately lower the heat to medium. Cook for around 10–15 minutes until the bottom is crisp and richly browned and the sides and centre have started to change texture – use a spatula or slice to gently lift it to check it is not burning. You will need to flip the farl to cook the other side . If you are cooking it whole, make sure it feels quite firm before you turn it, otherwise you will lose the shape if you turn it too quickly.

6. Flip the bread farl over and cook the other side for a further 10–15 minutes. It is fully cooked through when it is richly browned on both sides, crisp and sounds hollow when tapped. Serve warm, sliced and buttered. .

Halloumi Croutons

These aren't quite croutons (see opposite for how to make those), but they are delicious, crispy, slightly chewy cubes of hot, fried halloumi, which make a wonderful topping for a soup.

SERVES 4

- 1 block of halloumi (usually around 225g/8oz)
- 1–2 teaspoons sunflower or rapeseed oil

1. Pat the halloumi block dry using kitchen paper to absorb any moisture then cut into even-sized cubes, around 1–2cm (½–¾in).
2. Warm the oil in a frying pan over a medium–high heat and add the cubes of halloumi. Fry for around 3–5 minutes, turning each cube so that every side cooks evenly and takes on a golden colour and some crispy texture.

★ These are best served pretty much straight out of the pan, so cook them at the very last minute before serving, as they won't be at their best for long.

Homemade Croutons

Croutons are such a nice way to garnish a bowl of soup, and an ideal use for stale bread. Homemade croutons are in a different league from anything you can buy, and that's partly down to freshness – they really are best made on demand.

Stale bread
Olive oil
Salt

1. Cut, or tear up, the bread into evenly sized pieces. For softer-textured sliced bread, cutting it into small cubes with a knife may be the best option. If I have firm, rustic-style bread, I usually tear it into chunks.

   I have a couple of ways of making croutons:

   Pan-fry

   This method tends to be easier if you have cubes of bread, rather than rough chunks. Warm 1 tablespoon of olive oil in a large frying pan over a medium–high heat. Add the bread and fry, turning the cubes regularly, until golden brown and crisp. Keep an eye on the heat to ensure the bread is crisping not burning. Remove from the pan and drain on kitchen paper, if needed. Season with a sprinkle of salt and serve.

   Oven-bake

   This method can produce more successful results with roughly shaped chunks of firm bread, such as sourdough or artisanal loaves. Preheat the oven to 180°C/160°C fan (350°F), Gas Mark 4. Put the pieces of bread on a baking tray, drizzle with olive oil and sprinkle with salt. Bake for 5–15 minutes, checking the croutons every few minutes, and turning them as they cook. When they are golden brown and crisp, remove them from the oven and allow to cool a little before serving.

★ Croutons are best freshly made, but will store in an airtight container for 5 days.

8

Building Blocks

Homemade Vegetable Stock

Once you get into the habit of making stock, it really doesn't take much effort, just a little time when you are around at home. It freezes wonderfully, but do measure it and label your bags or boxes, which you will find very helpful when you come to use the stock. Don't be tempted to add salt until you come to use the stock in one of the soup recipes.

MAKES AROUND 1 LITRE (1¾ PINTS)

1 unpeeled onion, halved
1 leek, halved lengthways (or use the trimmed tops from leeks, which you can store in the freezer for this purpose)
2 celery sticks, halved
2 carrots, halved
2 bay leaves
1 teaspoon peppercorns
Small bunch of fresh thyme, or some fresh parsley stalks
1 litre (1¾ pints) water

1. Place all the ingredients into a large saucepan or stockpot. If the vegetables are not fully submerged, add a little more water. Simmer gently, uncovered, for an hour. Cool then strain (I do this by pouring through a sieve or colander into a large mixing bowl).

★ The stock can be used straight away, or chilled and used within 5 days, or frozen until required.

A

Homemade Chicken Stock

This is a lovely stock to prepare when you have some chicken bones to hand. After you've roasted a chicken, strip off the meat for your meal and use the roasted carcass to make stock. Otherwise, ask your butcher for bones: many will happily give you some for free or a small contribution. This is a recipe that will happily scale up if you have more bones, so it's worth making a batch. For best results, leave the stock to simmer for up to 3 hours and be sure not to add any salt. Like vegetable stock, this freezes wonderfully: remember to measure it and label your bags or boxes – you'll be glad you did when you come to use the stock in recipes.

MAKES AROUND 1 LITRE (1¾ PINTS)

1 chicken carcass or 500g (1lb 2oz) bones (raw or roasted), skin and wing tips removed

1 unpeeled onion, halved

1 leek, halved lengthways (or use the trimmed tops from leeks, which you can store in the freezer for this purpose)

1 celery stick

1 carrot, halved

2 bay leaves

1 teaspoon peppercorns

1 litre (1¾ pints) water

1. Put all the ingredients into a large saucepan, or stockpot, over a medium heat. If the carcass and vegetables are not fully submerged, add a little more water. Simmer gently, uncovered, for 1–3 hours. Cool and strain (I pour it through a sieve or colander into a large mixing bowl).

★ The stock can be used straight away, or chilled and stored in the fridge for 5 days or frozen until required.

Dashi

Dashi is a Japanese stock made from fish and seaweed. The ingredients required to make this staple recipe are widely available from specialist shops and online retailers. Kombu (dried seaweed) comes in sheets, which can be cut or broken to size. Bonito flakes are made from dried skipjack tuna and are often smoked and fermented. These fine flakes add a wonderful richness and depth of flavour – I encourage you to try them.

MAKES AROUND 1 LITRE (1¾ PINTS)

20g (¾oz) dried kelp seaweed (kombu), broken into pieces to fit the pan

1 litre (1¾ pints) water

20g (¾oz) dried bonito flakes (katsuobushi)

1. Rinse the kombu under cold water. Add to a large saucepan with the water and bonito flakes. Bring to a simmer over a medium heat and allow to simmer gently for 30 minutes. Stir well and leave to cool.
2. Strain through a sieve or muslin cloth. The dashi can be used straight away or chilled and used within 5 days. Do not freeze.

Simple Miso Soup

This is a wonderfully simple, savoury soup. It is fantastic enjoyed hot and forms a nice base recipe to which you could add other ingredients, such as kombu and silken tofu cubes.

MAKES AROUND 1 LITRE (1¾ PINTS)

1 litre (1¾ pints) dashi (see opposite)

100g (3½oz) red or brown miso paste

1. Pour the dashi into a large saucepan over a medium heat and bring to a gentle simmer. Add the miso paste, whisk until the two are evenly mixed and the soup is hot.
2. Serve immediately or allow to cool and store for up to 5 days in the fridge. This soup will reheat well.

Roasted Onion Soup Base

This simple soup base can be such a helpful shortcut when time is limited. Often, much of the time needed to make a soup is spent gently softening onions at the start of a recipe. Instead, you can get ahead by roasting them until they are meltingly soft and sweet. Having some ready-roasted onions to hand not only saves you time when you come to make a soup but they will add a wonderful savoury flavour and a pleasingly silky finish. Feel free to cook the quantities you need. I make this soup base in one of two ways: either as a very large batch spread over two trays to fill the oven, or on one tray, which I do when I am already using the oven for something else. I find that batch-cooking these onions and freezing them in 175g (6oz) portions works really well, which is the equivalent of 1 medium–large onion in a recipe.

Onions, sliced
Olive oil
Salt and freshly ground pepper

1. Preheat the oven to 180°C/160°C fan (350°F), Gas Mark 4.
2. Put the sliced onions on a baking tray. Drizzle with a little oil and season lightly with salt and pepper. Toss together to ensure the onions are coated with oil and seasoning. Cover the tray with foil, then roast for 20–40 minutes, checking regularly and turning the onions at intervals to ensure they cook evenly, until tender and succulent.
3. Remove from the oven, cool and either refrigerate for up to 5 days or freeze. The onions can be added to the pan with the rest of the ingredients required for the recipe, topped up with hot stock and cooked as per the method. Add them chilled, defrosted or frozen, if you're really tight on time.

V

Batch-Cooked Soup Base

This is a variation on the roasted onion soup base and gives you the option of being able to make soups in less time and with less effort on a regular basis. Cooking the base ingredients in the oven saves time compared with slowly softening them in a pan, and is ideal for cooking ingredients in batches to make a large quantity of soup, or if you want to make soups on a regular basis. This recipe is a guide, so feel free to scale up or down to suit your needs. You can use the vegetables you require for your favourite recipes, although this trio is a classic combination that works in a great number of recipes. You could separate the ingredients to freeze separately, or keep them mixed together. Aim for around 450g (1lb) of roasted vegetables to form the base of a soup.

2 onions, sliced

2 carrots, diced

2 celery sticks, trimmed and sliced

Olive oil

Salt and freshly ground pepper

1. Preheat the oven to 180°C/160°C fan (350°F), Gas Mark 4.
2. Put the onions, carrots and celery on a baking tray. Drizzle with a little oil and season lightly with salt and pepper. Toss together to ensure the vegetables are evenly coated with oil and seasoning. Cover the tray with foil, then roast for 20–40 minutes, checking regularly and turning the vegetables at intervals to ensure they cook evenly, until tender and succulent.
3. Remove from the oven, cool and either refrigerate for up to 5 days or freeze. They can be added to a pan with the rest of the ingredients required for the recipe, topped up with hot stock and cooked as per the method. Add them chilled, defrosted or even frozen, if you're really tight on time.

Index

A

ajo blanco 44–5
almonds, in ajo blanco 44
apple
&beetroot soup 134
onion & thyme soup 70–1
avocado 108

B

bacon
crispy sprinkles 62, 143
rice & bean soup 100–1
basil
in herb oil 145
pesto 140
tomato & coconut soup 130
beans, black
Cuban-inspired soup 66–7
rice & bacon soup 100–1
tomato & lime soup, with avocado & totopos 108–9
beans, butter
chorizo & cabbage soup 110–11
& red pepper soup 68–9
beans, cannellini
kale & lemon broth 78
spring greens broth 84
beans, edamame, in miso soup 28
beans, haricot, kale & lemon broth 78
beansprouts 106
beef, pearl barley & tomato soup 86–7
beetroot
& apple soup, roasted 134–5
ginger & lime soup 96–7
bessara 116–17
blended soups 10
blenders, using 10, 11
blue cheese & butternut squash soup 126–7
boiling, avoiding 10, 14
bonito flakes, in dashi 162
Brazilian-inspired soup, rice, bean & bacon 100–1
bread
in ajo blanco 44
cheesy wheaten farls 154–5
croutons 157
flatbreads 147
focaccia 151–3
fougasse 148–50
in gazpacho 40
budget soups 8, 52–71
building blocks 9, 160–5
butternut squash
& blue cheese soup 126–7
& coconut soup 136–7
& lentil spiced soup 118–19
& rosemary soup 128
in vegetable soup 74

C

cabbage, chorizo & butter bean soup 110–11
carrot
batch-cooked soup base 165
beef, pearl barley & tomato soup 86
bessara 116
in chicken soup 76
& coriander seed soup 60–1
cumin & honey-roasted soup 131
ginger & orange soup 83
lentil & tahini soup 92–3
roasted root vegetable soup 132
in stock 160, 161
turkey & barley soup 114
in vegetable soup 74
cauliflower & chickpea spiced soup 112–13
celeriac & leek soup 120
celery
batch-cooked soup base 165
beef, pearl barley & tomato soup 86
beetroot & apple soup 134
bessara 116
in chicken soup 76
in kale, bean & lemon broth 78
& leek soup 57

in stock 160, 161
turkey & barley soup 114
in vegetable soup 74
chard, broth 84
Cheddar cheese
cheese scones 146
cheesy wheaten farls 154–5
cheese *see* Cheddar; halloumi; parmesan etc.
chicken
get better soup 76–7
& ginger meatball broth 102
lemon orzo soup 58
with ramen 106
stock 161
& sweetcorn soup 82
Thai coconut noodle broth 20
chickpea
& cauliflower spiced soup 112–13
tomatoes & spinach soup 22–3
chilli flakes, crispy chilli oil 145
chorizo, butter bean & cabbage soup 110–11
coconut milk
full-fat 10
roasted tomato & basil soup 130
& squash soup 136
sweet potato & lemongrass soup 94
Thai coconut noodle broth 20
cold soups 8, 11
consistency of soup 11
coriander (leaves)
as garnish 20, 66, 90, 100, 116
ginger chicken meatball broth 102
in herb oil 145
coriander (seed)
butternut squash & lentil soup 118
carrot, lentil & tahini soup 92
& carrot soup 60–1
lentil, tomato & ras-el-hanout soup 90
cream
in chicken soup 76
chicken & sweetcorn soup 82
chilled creamy pea soup 38–9
full-fat 10
as garnish 15
in onion, apple & thyme soup 70
in potato soup 52
in watercress soup 43
crème fraîche, as garnish 15
croutons
as garnish 15
halloumi 156
homemade 157
Cuban-inspired soup, black bean 66–7
cucumber
chilled soup with tahini 42
in gazpacho 40
in hiyajiru 46
watermelon & lime soup 47
& yogurt chilled soup 48–9

D

dashi 46, 162, 163

E

edamame beans, in miso soup 28
eggs, with ramen 106
equipment 11

F

fennel (bulb), in vegetable soup 74
finishing touches 9, 140–57
fish
soup, with tomatoes & white wine 34
stock, dashi 46, 162, 163
flasks, for soup 14
flatbreads, fluffy puffy 147
focaccia 151–3
food mill 11
fougasse 148–50
freezing soup 14
frozen vegetables 10

G

garlic
- black bean soup 66
- cooking 10, 176
- lentil & lemon soup 26
- lentil & mint soup 55
- roasted 128
- yogurt 55, 144

garnishes 15
gazpacho 40–1
Ghanaian-inspired soup, sweet potato, ginger & peanut 104–5
ginger
- beetroot & lime soup 96–7
- butternut squash & lentil 116
- carrot, lentil & tahini soup 92
- carrot & orange soup 83
- chicken meatball broth 102
- & swede soup 56
- sweet potato & peanut soup 104–5

glossary 174

H

halloumi croutons 156
harissa & parsnip soup 64–5
healthy soups 8
herbs
- as garnish 15
- herb oil 145

hiyajiru 46
hot & sour soup with prawns & noodles 24–5

I

ingredients 12–13
Italian-inspired recipes
- focaccia 151–3
- pasta in brodo 32
- polentina 62–3

J

Japanese-inspired soup
- dashi 46, 162, 163
- hiyajiru 46
- ramen 106–7

just what the doctor ordered soups 8, 74–97

K

kale
- broth 84
- as garnish 62
- in vegetable soup 74
- white bean & lemon broth 78–9

key 7

L

labelling soup 14
leek
- & celeriac soup 120
- & celery soup 57
- in chicken soup 76
- creamy potato soup 52
- spring greens broth 84
- in stock 160, 161
- in vegetable soup 74

leftovers, using 13
lemon orzo soup 58–9
lemongrass, sweet potato & coconut soup 94–5
lentils, green, garlic & mint soup 55
lentils, red
- & butternut squash spiced soup 118–19
- carrot & tahini soup 92
- lemon & garlic soup 26
- tomato & ras-el-hanout soup 90–1
- turmeric & lemon soup 80–1

lettuce & spring onion soup 54
Levantine-inspired soup, chilled 48
lime 47, 96, 102, 108

M

measurements 176
meat, using leftovers 13
meatballs, chicken & ginger 102
Mexican-inspired soup, bean, tomato & lime, with avocado & totopos 108–9
microwave heating 13, 14
milk
- in celery & leek soup 57
- in cheese scones 146
- cheesy wheaten farls 154
- in potato soup 52
- in sweetcorn chowder 35

mint 48, 55
mirin 46
miso, brown
  miso soup 163
  ramen 106–7
miso, red
  hiyajiru 46
  miso soup 163
  ramen 106–7
miso, white, with udon, edamame & salmon 28–9
Moroccan-inspired soup, bessara 116–17
mouli-légumes 11

N

nigella seeds, toasted seed mix 144
no-cook soups 8, 38–49
noodles
  egg, in hot & sour soup 24–5
  ramen 106–7
  Thai coconut noodle broth 20
  udon, in miso soup 28
  see also pasta

O

office, taking soup to 14
oil
  crispy chilli 145
  as garnish 15
  herb 145
olive oil
  in focaccia 151
  in pesto 140
olives, black 121
onions
  apple & thyme soup 70–1
  cooking 10
  roasted soup base 164, 165
  in stock 160, 161
  see also spring onions
orange, carrot & ginger soup 83
orzo
  & lemon soup 58
  pasta in brodo 32
oven-baked soups 9, 124–37

P

pak choi, with ramen 106
Parmesan
  in pesto 140
  polentina 62
  uses for rinds 10
  vegetarian 176
Parmigiano Reggiano
  kale, bean & lemon broth 78
  lemon orzo soup 58
  pasta in brodo soup 32
  using rinds 10, 32
parsley
  as garnish 34, 90
  in herb oil 145
  & pea soup 27
  pesto 52, 140, 142
  spring greens broth 84
  in stock 160
parsnip
  & harissa soup 64–5
  roasted root vegetable soup 132–3
  rosemary & olive soup 121
pasta
  lemon orzo soup 58
  pasta in brodo, with peas & Parmesan 32–3
  spinach & yogurt soup 88–9
peanut butter, sweet potato & ginger soup 104–5
pearl barley
  beef & tomato soup 86–7
  turkey & vegetable soup 114–15
peas
  chilled creamy pea soup 38–9
  pasta in brodo soup 32–3
  pea & parsley soup 27
peas, split, in bessara 116
pepper, white 10
peppers, red
  & butter bean soup 68–9
  Cuban-inspired soup 66
  in gazpacho 40
  in vegetable soup 74
pesto
  basil 140
  as garnish 15
  parsley 52, 140, 142
  pumpkin seed 142

pine nuts
in pesto 140
toasted seed mix 144
polentina 62–3
poppy seeds, toasted seed mix 144
pork, with ramen 106
potato
in celery & leek soup 57
chicken & sweetcorn soup 82
creamy potato soup 52–3
in swede & ginger soup 56
in sweetcorn chowder 35
to reduce oversalting 11
prawns, in hot & sour soup 24–5
presentation tips 15
pumpkin
& lentil spiced soup 118
& rosemary soup 128–9
see also butternut squash
pumpkin seed
pesto 142
toasted seed mix 144

Q

quick soups 8, 20–35

R

ramen 106–7
ras-el-hanout 90
recipe quantities 15
reducing soup 11
reheating soup 10, 14
rice, bean & bacon soup 100–1
rice noodles 20
rosemary 121, 128, 145

S

salmon
in fish soup 34
in miso soup 28
salt, reducing oversalting 11
scones, cheese 146
seasoning 10
seaweed 46, 106, 162
serving tips 15
sesame oil, in ramen 106
sesame seeds
in ramen 106
toasted seed mix 144
shallots 40, 47, 48
simmer, importance of 10
soup
bases 9, 164, 165
keeping warm 15
oversalted 11
presentation tips 15
reducing 11
reheating 10, 14
splitting 10
storing 14
thickening 11
transporting 14
Spanish-inspired soup
ajo blanco 44–5
cauliflower, & chickpea spiced 112–13
chilled 40, 44
gazpacho 40
lentil, garlic & mint 55
spices, cooking whole 10
spinach
chickpea & tomato soup 22–3
pasta & yogurt soup 88–9
split peas, bessara 116
spring greens
bessara 116
broth 84–5
rice, bean & bacon soup 100
in vegetable soup 74
spring onions
& lettuce soup 54
pasta in brodo soup 32–3
with ramen 106
sweetcorn chowder 35
stock 9, 12
chicken 161
dashi 46, 162, 163
vegetable 160
storecupboard ingredients 12–13
storing soup 14
swede
& ginger soup 56

roasted root vegetable soup 132
sweet potato
ginger & peanut soup 104–5
lemongrass & coconut soup 94–5
sweetcorn
& chicken soup 82
chowder 35
with ramen 106
symbols 7

T

tahini
carrot & lentil soup 92
& cucumber soup 42
Thai basil 20
Thai-inspired soup
coconut noodle broth 20–1
ginger chicken meatball broth 102
squash & coconut 136–7
thickening soup 11
thyme, onion & apple soup 70–1
tips and tricks 10–11
tofu, silken
in hiyajiru 46
in ramen 106
tomatoes
bean, tomato & lime soup 108
beef & pearl barley soup 86–7
chickpea & spinach soup 22–3
chorizo, butter bean & cabbage soup 110
coconut & basil soup 130
in fish soup 34
foolproof tomato soup 30–1
in gazpacho 40
lentil & ras-el-hanout soup 90
red pepper & butter bean soup 68
sweet potato, ginger & peanut soup 104
in vegetable soup 74
totopos 108
transporting soup 14
turkey, barley & vegetable soup 114–15
turmeric 80, 118, 124

U

udon noodles, in miso soup 28

V

vegetables
peelings 12
preparation 176
roasting 10
stock 160
vegetable soup 74–5

W

watercress
chilled soup 43
with polentina 62
watermelon, cucumber & lime chilled soup 47
wellbeing 8
wine, white 34
winter warmers 9, 100–21
work, taking soup to 14

Y

yogurt
& cucumber chilled soup 48–9
in flatbreads 147
full-fat 10
garlic 55, 144
pasta & spinach soup 88–9

UK-US Glossary

bicarbonate of soda .... baking soda
butter beans .... lima beans
caster sugar .... superfine sugar
cavolo nero .... Tuscan kale
chickpeas .... garbanzo beans
chilli .... chile/chili pepper
coriander .... cilantro
double cream .... heavy cream
flaked almonds .... slivered almonds
hispi cabbage .... sweetheart cabbage
minced (meat) .... ground (meat)
pak choi .... bok choi
pepper (red/green/yellow) .... bell pepper
plain flour .... all-purpose flour
polenta .... cornmeal
prawns .... shrimp
rapeseed oil .... canola oil
rasher (of bacon) .... slice
self-raising flour .... self-rising flour
soured cream .... sour cream
spring onions .... scallions
stock .... broth
stock cubes .... bouillon cubes
swede .... rutabaga

Equipment

baking paper .... parchment paper
baking tin .... baking pan
clingfilm .... plastic wrap
frying pan .... skillet
grill .... broiler
jug .... pitcher
kitchen paper .... paper towels
roasting tray .... roasting pan
sieve .... strainer

Acknowledgements

Writing cookbooks has been a long-held dream of mine, and the very special privilege to write another book feels just as special on book number 7 as it did the first time.

I am deeply grateful to everyone who has been instrumental in making this book happen.

My agent, Elly James, has been a tremendous support to me and I truly appreciate your belief in me and my work. Kate Fox at Hamlyn commissioned this book and has been an absolute joy to work with – no-one could be more kind, fun and enthusiastic – thank you, Kate.

The whole team at Hamlyn have been a dream to work with and I am indebted to you all. Thank you Alice Gawthrop, Sybella Stephens, Jonathan Christie, Caroline Alberti, Ailie Springall and Erin Brown for being a delight.

Special thanks to Stephanie Evans who edited my manuscript so brilliantly and was simply wonderful to work with. Thank you for all your expertise, care and attention.

This book has been beautifully produced by the creative team, including Danielle Wood, Katy McClelland and Megan Thomson. Thank you for your hard work and creativity in producing this book.

I am profoundly grateful to everyone who continues to read and buy my work. I am continuously inspired to create recipes that work well and introduce new ideas to people's repertoires, so thank you to you for reading and cooking from my books.

Many thanks are due to my colleagues from around the world who have supported me in producing my work and writing about it.

And finally, thank you to my wonderful support network at home who help me in so many ways. Thank you to my wonderful friends, and Mum and Dad, Lucy and Andy, Jean and Tony. I appreciate everything you do for me.

First published in Great Britain in 2025 by Hamlyn,
an imprint of Octopus Publishing Group Ltd
Carmelite House
50 Victoria Embankment
London EC4Y 0DZ
www.octopusbooks.co.uk

An Hachette UK Company
www.hachette.co.uk

The authorized representative in the EEA is
Hachette Ireland, 8 Castlecourt Centre,
Dublin 15, D15 XTP3, Ireland (email: info@hbgi.ie)

Distributed in the US by Hachette Book Group
1290 Avenue of the Americas, 4th and 5th Floors,
New York, NY 10104

Distributed in Canada by Canadian Manda Group
664 Annette St., Toronto, Ontario,
Canada M6S 2C8

ISBN 978 0 60063 915 2

A CIP catalogue record for this book is available from the British Library.

Printed and bound in China.

10 9 8 7 6 5 4 3 2 1

Publisher: Kate Fox
Senior Managing Editor: Sybella Stephens
Editorial Assistant: Alice Gawthrop
Creative Director: Jonathan Christie
Photographer: Danielle Wood
Food Stylist: Katy McClelland
Props Stylist: Megan Thomson
Production Manager: Caroline Alberti

Standard level spoon measurements are used in all recipes:
1 tablespoon = one 15ml spoon
1 teaspoon = one 5ml spoon

Root vegetables, including potatoes, garlic and onions, are peeled unless otherwise stated; other vegetables are washed and trimmed.

Vegetarians should look for the 'V' symbol on a cheese to ensure it is made with vegetarian rennet. Parmigiano Reggiano, for example, is always made with animal-based rennet, but Parmesan-style vegetarian cheese is available.

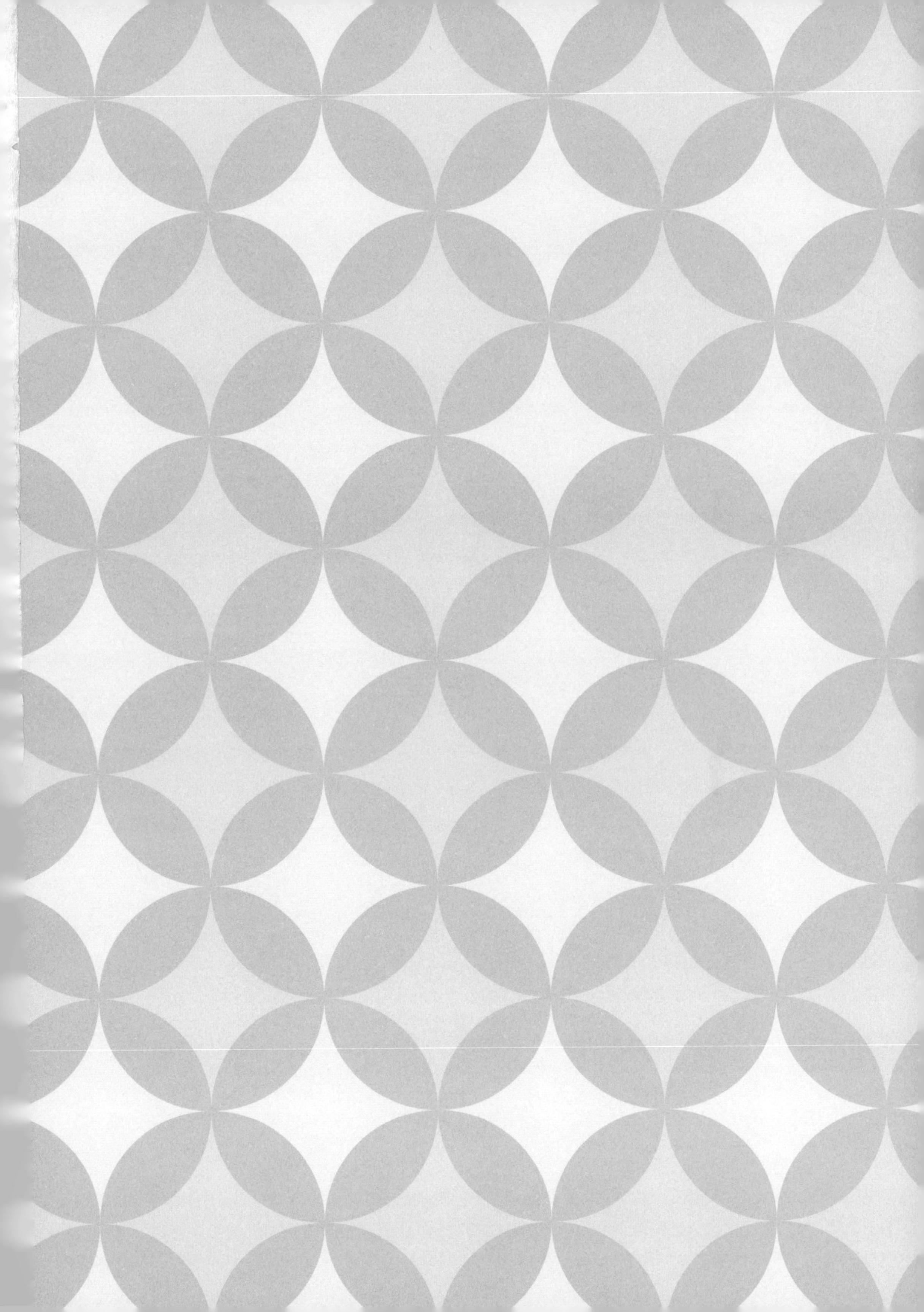